GIRLS ARE PEOPLE TOO!

A Bibliography of Nontraditional Female Roles in Children's Books

by

JOAN E. NEWMAN

THE SCARECROW PRESS, INC.
Metuchen, N.J., & London 1982

Library of Congress Cataloging in Publication Data

Newman, Joan E.
    Girls are people too!

    Includes bibliographical references and index.
    1. Children--Books and reading--Bibliography.
2. Women in literature--Bibliography. I. Title.
Z1037.N66   [PN1009.A1]   011'.62   81-18548
ISBN 0-8108-1500-1   AACR2

CONTENTS

INTRODUCTION

Though the problems resulting from rigidly assigned behavioral roles have only recently gained widespread recognition, the existence of the double standard based on gender has long been acknowledged. In 1898, Charlotte Perkins Gilman in Women and Economics wrote:

> Boys and girls are expected to behave differently to each other, and to people in general, --a behavior to be briefly described in two words. To the boy we say, "Do"; to the girl, "Don't."

Recent studies have shown that children's literature portrays females as passive, dependent, domestic, unimaginative, unathletic, incompetent, diffident, illogical, and timid. On the other hand, it depicts males as active, independent, authoritative, creative, athletic, capable, self-confident, logical, and adventurous, as well as aggressive, competitive, brave, persevering, and achieving. [1,2,3] The qualities that are positive and highly esteemed are represented by males, the negative and inferior traits by females.

Pamela E. Butler writes that the consequences of stereotyped femininity are: (1) reduced assertiveness--inability to control external influences in life, express anger, experience competency, and become a problem-solving human being; (2) emotional distress; (3) powerlessness; and (4) depression. [4]

Other authors insist that the detrimental results of sexism are even more extensive. In Sexism in Children's Books, the authors observe that both boys and girls suffer from rigid, standardized sex roles. Rigid sex-role definitions not only foster unhappiness in children, but they also hamper their fullest intellectual and social development. [5]

iv

According to Dan Donlan, picture books and other children's literature traditionally have three recurring female types: the sweet little old lady, the beautiful young heroine, and the independent woman. [6] The first type, the ineffectual old lady who is eccentric or befuddled, is well illustrated by the Amelia Bedelia and the Miss Pickerell series. These characters neither create the situations nor react with decisiveness, control, and consideration of the alternatives and consequences.

The second female type is the beautiful young heroine who is helplessly dependent upon men. This category is most frequently represented by fairy tales ("Cinderella," "Sleeping Beauty," and "Rapunzel"). Here the heroines are passive, naive, dull-witted, and spiritless.

The independent woman represents the third female image. This category is comprised of evil witches as in "Hansel and Gretel" and "Snow White," and hateful housewives, as in "The Fisherman and His Wife." Although these characters are powerful, they also connote the negative qualities of malevolence, dominance, and vengeance.

In these days of single-parent families, working mothers, househusbands, and live-in partners, children's literature should reflect the variety of role models available in the culture. This annotated bibliography of nontraditional female role models in children's literature explores these options.

The major criterion for inclusion in this selective list is the female character's nontraditionalism--that the characters are not only different, but also possess dignity and intelligence. To show successful human beings, I have cited books that exhibit active, adventurous, persistent, self-confident, independent, creative, proud, courageous, and individualistic females. The person who happens onto a situation and bumbles her way out is not considered an appropriate model for this selection of books. A listed book may contain some sexism or stereotyping, but if a protagonist for the most part plays a nontraditional role, then I have cited it.

In the same way, I have considered such traits as understanding, caring and concern for others, and emotional expressiveness to be appropriate female qualities. Consequently, this bibliography may not receive the unqualified approval of a strict feminist. My purpose has been to choose books that

reject neither feminism nor femaleness. This compilation re-
flects the opinion that it is still a female's right to be able to
choose a traditional or nontraditional role.

I have taken into consideration the time period depicted
in the literature when determining whether a character is nontraditional. If the female character's actions were considered
nontraditional, progressive, or radical in a particular period
(though they may seem commonplace by today's standards),
that book is included in the bibliography. For example, in
Master Rosalind (item 170), which takes place in the fourteenth
century, Rosalind must disguise herself, since it is illegal for
girls to be players or actresses.

The selection of books that follows was developed after
searching The Horn Book and Publishers Weekly; Charlotte
Huck's Children's Literature in the Elementary School, The
Book-Finder, and Enid Davis's The Liberty Cap; Little Miss
Muffet Fights Back, by Feminists on Children's Media; other
nonsexist and minority bibliographies; and the shelves of the
University of Iowa, Coralville, and Iowa City libraries. Li-
brarians of these institutions also made suggestions.

Books that display female and male cooperation on an
equal basis or females in a leadership position are listed.
Books by male and female authors are considered equally, although fewer than twenty percent of the selections are by male authors. Newer (within the last ten years) works of fiction published in the United States form the nucleus of the bibliography.
The age groups represented are primary (preschool-grade 3)
and intermediate (grades 4-9). The age levels are those sug-
gested by the publishers in Books in Print. These are to be
used only as general guides: the maturity of the individual
child should dictate the final selection. Fiction and nonfiction
are listed separately, as are books dealing with some minority groups (all too few of these have been published).

The appendix constitutes a unique feature: a chrono-
logy listing notable events and personalities in the history of
women. Women who have contributed to this history by being "the first," had a significant influence on the development of the female image, or gained notoriety for their non-
traditionalism are recorded. I have made an attempt to include minorities (race, age, and ability) where possible.
However, many of the achievements of these groups are not
well documented or publicized. Most of the listed events are
American, in keeping with the American emphasis of this
bibliography.

Those selections rated as "excellent" (**) offer an interesting, exciting plot that continues throughout the book; well-developed, realistic characters; a strong heroine who illustrates nontraditional female qualities or roles; an understandable, smooth reading style; illustrations that supplement and enhance the text in a picture book; and elements that are consistent with historical facts in nonfiction and historical fiction.

A "good" (*) rating indicates qualities similar to those judged excellent; however, these books lack the highly creative or unusual plots, consistently independent heroines, exceptional illustrations, or straightforward style.

A book judged to be "fair" may exhibit a plot that lags in places; a plot or characters who are not well-developed or entirely believable; a heroine who exhibits some stereotypical behavior, few nontraditional characteristics, or inconsistent behavior; or a dull or complicated writing style. All of these criteria might not be found in a "fair" book, but any combination of several of them will result in this rating.

The purpose of this bibliography is threefold. First, to stress that these are not books for girls only, but books about girls for young readers. If boys are acquainted with nontraditional females in literature, they may be more willing to accept nontraditional roles and qualities for themselves and others. Second, it is intended that this bibliography will aid parents, teachers, and librarians in selecting books to purchase and recommend for young readers. Third, although there are some nonsexist bibliographies available, most were completed in the early or middle seventies and none emphasizes the nontraditional aspects of female behavior. This compilation seeks to update the other bibliographies and approach children's literature from the perspective of accenting nontraditional role models.

NOTES

1. Margret Andersen, Mother Was Not a Person (Montreal: Content/Black Rose, 1972), p. 28.

2. Betty Levy, "The School's Role in the Sex-Role Stereotyping of Girls: A Feminist Review of the Literature," in Sexism and Youth, comp. by Diane Gersoni-Stavn (New York: Bowker, 1974), p. 50.

3. Women on Words and Images (Society), Dick and Jane as
Victims: Sex Stereotyping in Children's Readers (Princeton:
Women on Words and Images, 1975), p. 12.

4. Pamela E. Butler, Self-Assertion for Women: A Guide
to Becoming Androgynous* (*fully human) (San Francisco:
Harper & Row, 1976), p. 22.

5. Children's Rights Workshop, ed., Sexism in Children's
Books: Facts, Figures & Guidelines (London: Writers &
Readers, 1976), p. 18.

6. Dan Donlan, "The Negative Image of Women in Children's
Literature," in Sexism and Youth, comp. by Diane Gersoni-
Stavn (New York: Bowker, 1974), pp. 218-223, passim.

GIRLS ARE PEOPLE TOO!

A Bibliography of Nontraditional
Female Roles in Children's Books

---

1   *Abramovitz, Anita. Winifred. Austin, Tex. : Steck-
Vaughn, 1971. grades K-3
An inventive girl, Winifred makes things and gives
them as presents to everyone on her street. When a
neighbor suggests that she make signs, she complies
but is overzealous. However, Winifred is able to
solve her own problem and please others.

2   *Adler, David A. Cam Jansen and the Mystery of the
Stolen Diamonds. New York: Viking, 1980.
grades 2-5
While Cam and her friend Eric babysit for his brother,
they witness a burglary at the jewelry store. Cam
uses her photographic memory and helps solve the
robbery. This is one in a series of Cam Jansen mysteries.

3   *Aitken, Amy. Ruby! Scarsdale, N. Y. : Bradbury,
1979. grades K-2
In deciding to change her routine life, Ruby imagines
the excitement and fame she will receive when she becomes an author, artist, movie star, and President.

4   Aliki. At Mary Bloom's. New York: Morrow, 1976.
grades K-3
When a little girl's mouse has babies, she wants to
share the news with Mary Bloom, who helps her cele-
brate the birth of the mice with a party.

5   *Ardizzone, Edward. Diana and Her Rhinoceros. New
York: Walck, 1964. grades K-4
When a rhinoceros with a cold wanders into the Effing-
ham-Jones sitting room one night, Diana nurses it

back to health and refuses to let men from the zoo shoot it. She keeps it in a shed in the backyard where she can play with it and feed it.

6   *Asch, Frank. Gia and the One Hundred Dollars Worth of Bubblegum. New York: McGraw-Hill, 1974. grades K+
For befriending a dog, Gia receives $100, which she uses to buy bubblegum. Gia and her friends blow huge bubbles that carry them into the air. When a seagull breaks the bubble, the gull gives them a ride around the world and drops them off at the circus.

7   *Babbitt, Natalie. Phoebe's Revolt. New York: Farrar, Straus & Giroux, 1968. grades Preschool-3
Told in verse, this story depicts a little girl at the turn of the century in Manhattan who wants to wear simple, unadorned clothes like her father instead of ribbons and clothes with frills. Unable to dissuade her, Phoebe's parents finally allow her to wear her father's clothes for a week. However, Phoebe's father ingeniously maneuvers his wife into seeing Phoebe's point on informal clothes.

8   *Baker, Betty. Latki and the Lightning Lizard. New York: Macmillan, 1979. grades K-3
The youngest of four sisters, Latki is especially fond of Seri, her next-older sister. When their woodcutter father chops down a lizard's home, the lizard demands that one of the woodcutter's daughters cook and clean for him. Seri goes, but Latki misses her sister and rescues her from the lizard.

9   **Baldwin, Anne Norris. Jenny's Revenge. New York: Four Winds, 1974. grades K-3
Unhappy that her mother works, Jenny tries several ways to make her babysitter quit so her mother will have to stay home. However, Jenny finally discovers that her behavior has been terrible and accepts her mother's need to work.

10   Bemelmans, Ludwig. Madeline. New York: Simon & Schuster, 1939. grades K-3
Living in a convent in France, Madeline shows that she is unafraid of mice, lions, and having her appendix removed. Madeline is the first in a series.

11   **Berenstain, Stan and Jan. He Bear, She Bear. New
        York: Random House, 1974. grades Preschool-
        1
      In addition to being a he bear and a she bear, and
      potentially a father and a mother, a brother and a
      sister bear speculate on all the things they can be
      whether they are he or she.

12   *Blaine, Marge. The Terrible Thing That Happened at
        Our House. New York: Parents' Magazine,
        1975. grades Preschool-3
      A little girl describes what happened at her house when
      her mother returned to teaching. However, with every-
      one's cooperation and schedule changes, things weren't
      so terrible any more.

13   **Bonsall, Crosby. And I Mean It, Stanley. New York:
        Harper & Row, 1974. grades Preschool-3
      A little girl talks to someone on the other side of the
      fence as she plays by herself and creates her junk
      masterpiece. Cleverly, she says that she doesn't want
      to play with him and won't let him see her creation so
      as to lure him from behind the fence.

14   *Bottner, Barbara. Messy. New York: Delacorte,
        1979. grades Preschool-3
      Harry, whose real name is Harriet, "must be the
      messiest child in town." Being messy is the only way
      she can find things. However, for a week before her
      dancing class recital, Harry is neat. But, after the
      recital, she is "messy again."

15   *Bottner, Barbara. There Was Nobody There. New
        York: Macmillan, 1978. grades Preschool-1
      When a little girl wakes up in the night and thinks
      she is alone, she imagines herself in many adventures
      --shipping out to sea, arriving at the North Pole,
      riding in a hot air balloon, and landing on the moon.

16   Brown, Beatrice Curtis. The Tale of Polly Polloo.
        New York: Seabury, 1969. grades Preschool-
        3
      When Miss Polly Polloo, who is as tall as a tree,
      takes a house to market, the townspeople get very
      upset. Polly decides to move to the country, but the
      people of the town miss Polly's excitement and ask her
      to return.

17 **Brown, Margaret Wise. The Steamroller. New
York: Walker, 1974. grades Preschool-2
For Christmas, Daisy receives a steamroller from
her parents. However, as she drives it down the
road, she discovers that she can't stop it and flat-
tens some animals and people. Just before the
steamroller falls into the ocean, she jumps off.
In order to solve the problem of the squashed things,
Daisy uses a giant steam shovel to scoop them up.

18 *Burnett, Carol. What I Want to Be When I Grow
Up--. New York: Simon & Schuster, 1975.
grades 1+
A variety of unusual careers are illustrated with
children's drawings and photographs of Carol Burnett.

19 *Burningham, John. Come Away from the Water,
Shirley. New York: Crowell, 1977. grades
1-2
While her parents relax on the beach, Shirley enjoys her own creative adventures--battling pirates,
walking the plank, and digging for buried treasure.

20 *Calhoun, Mary. Euphonia and the Flood. New
York: Parents' Magazine, 1976. grades K-
3
Euphonia has a motto: "If a thing is worth doing,
it's worth doing well." When a flood rises to her
doorstep, Euphonia decides to find out where it is
going. Unconcerned about her safety, she em-
barks on an exploration in her rowboat with her
pig and broom, rescues some animals, and arrives
at the flood's destination (a picnic).

21 Censoni, Robert. Cowgirl Kate. New York: Holiday House, 1977. grades Preschool-3
Living in a city apartment doesn't stop Kate from
pretending she is a cowgirl. Her western adventures make her week exciting. But by the end of
the week she is ready to change occupations again,
and she becomes a sailor.

22 *Chasek, Judith. Have You Seen Wilhelmina Krumpf?
New York: Lothrop, Lee & Shepard, 1973.
grades 1-5
In Poulderpoort, Holland, the women do almost
everything in exactly the same way as their grand-

mothers did. So, when Wilhelmina Krumpf begins
leaving her house instead of washing her windows,
the other housewives become curious and determined
to discover her secret errand. Following her one
afternoon, they are astonished to find her gaily
riding a motorcycle down the dike. However, when
Wilhelmina offers them a ride, they accept and discover that things do not have to remain the same.

23   *Chorao, Kay. A Magic Eye for Ida. New York:
            Seabury, 1973. grades 1-3
      Ida feels that no one is interested in her, so she
      decides to run away from home. She meets a for-
      tune-teller who tells her that she has something
      special. Reassured, Ida returns home to find her
      place in the world. Ida Makes a Movie is a sequel.

24   *Chorao, Kay. Molly's Moe. New York: Seabury,
            1976. grades K-3
      Molly wonders if her "brain is full of noodles," as
      her mother says. She seems to lose things quite
      easily. When she loses Moe, her stuffed stegosau-
      rus, Molly finds him and other misplaced things
      through systematic deduction and discovers that her
      brain is not "full of noodles." Molly's Lies is a
      sequel.

25   **Cole, Brock. No More Baths. Garden City, N.Y.:
            Doubleday, 1980. grades Preschool-3
      Spunky Jessie McWhistle decides to run away from
      home when she is asked to take a bath in the mid-
      dle of the day. She visits her friends who do not
      have to take baths--a chicken, a cat, and a pig.
      She tries each animal's way to get clean, but finds
      that their ways don't work for her. She returns
      home to take her own bath, still maintaining that
      there is nothing worse than a bath.

26   *Conford, Ellen. Impossible, Possum. Boston:
            Little, Brown, 1971. grades 1-3
      A young possum, Randolph is unable to hang upside
      down by his tail. However, Geraldine, his sister,
      finds a way to give Randolph self-confidence so he
      can hang by his tail without help.

27   *Conford, Ellen. Just the Thing for Geraldine.
            Boston: Little, Brown, 1974. grades 1-3

Geraldine loves to hang by her tail and juggle. Because her parents say there is more to life than
juggling, they send her to classes for ballet, weav-
ing, and sculpting. When none of these classes are
suitable, her parents finally decide to let her do
what she wants--juggle. This is a sequel to Impossible, Possum.

28 **Coombs, Patricia. Molly Mullett. New York:
Lothrop, Lee & Shepard, 1975. grades 1-4
When a greedy and troublesome Ogre steals food
and gold from the village, Molly bravely decides to
get them back herself. She succeeds in returning
one sack of gold, but the king orders Mr. Mullett
to get rid of the Ogre altogether. So, Molly must
return for the Ogre's sword, believed to be his
source of strength. Molly succeeds in this task
also and is knighted for her bravery.

29 Cutler, Ivor. Elephant Girl. New York: Morrow,
1976. grades K-3
Digging in her back yard, Balooky Klujypop uncovers
a real elephant. Balooky washes it in the kitchen
sink, dries it in the sun, and rides it in the garden
and house before she buries it once again in the
yard.

30 *Dalgliesh, Alice. The Courage of Sarah Noble.
New York: Scribner, 1954. grades 1-4
In 1707, eight-year-old Sarah goes with her father
from Massachusetts to Connecticut to cook for him
while he builds the log cabin for their family. Indians live just across the river from them, so the
Indian children and Sarah visit and play with each
other. When Sarah's father needs to bring the rest
of the family to the new house, Sarah stays with an
Indian family always mindful of her mother's words
--"Keep up your courage."

31 **de Paola, Tomie. Helga's Dowry: A Troll Love
Story. New York: Harcourt Brace Jovanovich, 1977. grades K-3
Determined to earn her own dowry in order to get
married, Helga sets out to acquire cattle, gold,
and land by working. However, when she returns,
Helga finds that her sweetheart has not waited for
her. She finds true love and marries another man,

who loves her for what she is, not for what she
has.

32   *de Regniers, Beatrice Schenk. <u>Laura's Story.</u> New
            York: Atheneum, 1979. grades Preschool-1
       Laura tells her mother a bedtime story about when
       she was big and her mother was little. In the story,
       Laura's mother is eaten by a fish, which is eaten
       by a dog, and so on, until her mother is finally
       able to rescue herself.

33   Devlin, Wende and Harry. <u>Cranberry Mystery.</u>
            New York: Parents' Magazine, 1978. grades
            Preschool-3
       When antiques begin disappearing in Cranberryport,
       the townspeople become concerned. After Mr.
       Whiskers's figurehead is stolen, he and Maggie are
       determined to catch the thieves themselves. Maggie's
       quick thinking, independence, and courage lead to the
       solution of the mystery.

34   *Devlin, Wende and Harry. <u>Hang On, Hester!</u> New
            York: Lothrop, Lee & Shepard, 1980. grades
            1-4
       Hester dreams of doing important things and being
       famous. When a flood carries her house down the
       river, Hester gets her chance by courageously hang-
       ing on to the house.

35   *Dragonwagon, Crescent. <u>When Light Turns into</u>
            <u>Night.</u> New York: Harper & Row, 1975.
            all ages
       Just before night falls, Ellen takes a walk away
       from "people places" to places where there are
       only grass, sky, wind, and birds. Here, she
       thinks about a variety of places ("people places
       and not people places") where she feels secure and
       satisfied, knowing that people are different.

36   *Dragonwagon, Crescent. <u>Will It Be Okay?</u> New
            York: Harper & Row, 1977. grades K-3
       A little girl asks questions about dogs, snakes,
       storms, love, death, and other things. Her mother
       shows her understanding and acceptance of the many
       fears of childhood with her patient answers.

37   Duncan, Jane. <u>Brave Janet Reachfar.</u> New York:

Seabury, 1975. grades K-2
Wanting to help get the sheep down from the hills
in a sudden snowstorm, Janet Reachfar goes to the
East Hill with her dog. When one sheep is missing,
she goes to look for it. Janet finds that the sheep
has a lamb and has caught her leg in the barbed wire
fence. Janet stays with the sheep, keeps the lamb
warm, and sends a hair ribbon with her dog to get
the family's hired hands.

38   Eber, Christine Engla. Just Momma and Me.
        Chapel Hill, N.C.: Lollipop Power, 1975.
        grades Preschool-3
An adopted girl enjoys being in a family of just her
momma and herself. Her mother, an artist, spends
time doing things together with her. One day, Karl
moves in with them. The little girl wishes it were
just the two of them again. When her mother has
a baby, the little girl thinks how her family has
grown and enjoys being a part of it.

39   *Ets, Marie Hall. Come Play with Me. Garden
        City, N.Y.: Puffin, 1955. grades Preschool-
        1
A little girl goes into the woods looking for someone
to play with her. She meets a bug, frog, snake,
and other animals and asks them to play with her,
but they run away. In frustration, she finally sits
down on a log and is rewarded for her patience
when the animals return to play with her.

40   **Freeman, Jean Todd. Cynthia and the Unicorn.
        New York: Norton, 1967. grades 1-6
Just before Christmas, Cynthia tells her parents
that she wants a unicorn. Already having a gryphon,
a troll, and a mermaid, she asks them for advice
on catching a unicorn, but they do not have very
useful suggestions. However, Christmas morning
brings Cynthia her wish in an unexpected way when
she receives a pony (a unicorn without a horn).

41   *Gaeddert, LouAnn. Noisy Nancy Norris. Garden
        City, N.Y.: Doubleday, 1965. grades Pre-
        school-3
Whenever Nancy does anything, it's always with
noise. When the landlady asks the family to move
unless there is complete peace and quiet, Nancy

quiets her activities at home. However, things are
unnaturally quiet, and the landlady asks for just a
little noise so she knows Nancy is all right. Nancy
is happy to comply. Noisy Nancy and Nick is a
sequel.

42   Gage, Wilson. Mrs. Gaddy and the Ghost. New
            York: Morrow, 1979. grades 1-4
        Mrs. Gaddy tries to get rid of the ghost that keeps
        her awake but finally decides that a ghost can be
        very good company.

43   *Galdone, Joanna. The Little Girl and the Big Bear.
            New York: Houghton Mifflin, 1980. grades
            Preschool-3
        In this retelling of a traditional Slavic tale, a little
        girl outwits the bear who is holding her captive.
        By hiding in a basket of pies, the girl is able to
        safely return to her grandparents.

44   **Gauch, Patricia Lee. Christina Katerina & the
            Box. New York: Coward, McCann & Geoghe-
            gan, 1971. grades K-3
        Christina loves empty boxes. When a refrigerator
        arrives for her mother, Christina promptly claims
        the box, which she transforms into a castle, a club
        house, a race car, and a ballroom floor.

45   Glovach, Linda. Hey, Wait for Me! I'm Amelia.
            Englewood Cliffs, N.J.: Prentice-Hall, 1971.
            grades K-4
        Amelia has nothing to do this Saturday, so she takes
        a train trip by herself into the city.

46   *Goffstein, M.B. Fish for Supper. New York: Dial,
            1976. grades Preschool-2
        Being a different kind of grandmother, this grand-
        mother spends her day fishing.

47   Goffstein, M.B. My Crazy Sister. New York:
            Dial, 1976. grades Preschool-3
        Although two sisters have different lifestyles, they
        show that they can live together and enjoy each other's
        company.

48   *Goffstein, M.B. Two Piano Tuners. New York:
            New York: Farrar, Straus & Giroux,
            1970. grades Preschool-3

Debbie lives with her grandfather, the best piano tuner in the world. So that she can become a concert pianist, Mr. Weinstock gives his granddaughter piano lessons. However, Debbie is determined to be a piano tuner and finds a way to convince her grandfather of her intentions and skill.

49   *Goins, Ellen H. <u>She Was Scared Silly</u>. Austin,
        Tex.: Steck-Vaughn, 1971. grades Preschool-
        2
From the moment Josephine wakes up in the morning, her imagination creates all sorts of animals and goblins to scare her silly--but not really, since she continues creating.

50   *Greenberg, Barbara. <u>The Bravest Babysitter</u>. New
        York: Dial, 1977. grades Preschool-3
Heather comes to babysit for Lisa, but when a thunderstorm scares Heather, they change roles. Lisa becomes the babysitter.

51   *Greenwald, Sheila. <u>The Hot Day</u>. Indianapolis:
        Bobbs-Merrill, 1972. grades 1-4
In the days before air conditioning, most people in the city sit outside to get cool. A few people have fans. In Sadie's family, they suffer through the heat while their boarder owns a fan. One night while her parents and their boarder are out, Sadie discovers a way to keep them cool.

52   **Grifalconi, Ann. <u>The Matter with Lucy: An Album.</u>
        Indianapolis: Bobbs-Merrill, 1973. all ages
At the turn of the century, Lucy is kept so busy helping her mother and older brothers that no one realizes that she dreams of going to school, where someone can teach her how to find the answers to her questions. With her determination, she is able to become a world-famous scholar.

53   Haas, Irene. <u>The Maggie B</u>. New York: Atheneum,
        1975. grades Preschool-3
Margaret gets her wish to sail for a day on a boat named after her with someone nice for company.

54   *Haley, Gail E. <u>The Abominable Swamp Man.</u> New
        York: Viking, 1975. grades 1-4
Complaints from citizens and fears that the Swamp

Man will hurt the tourist trade cause the sheriff
and his posse to try to catch him. Edwardina fears
for the life of the Swamp Man and ventures into the
swamp alone to warn him of the danger. After
finding and talking with him, Edwardina discovers
the pathway to another world--the world of magic--
and accompanies the Swamp Man there.

55   Hall, Rosalys. Miranda's Dragon. New York:
         McGraw-Hill, 1968. grades K-4
While strolling through the woods, Miranda and the
barber encounter a dragon. The barber runs away,
leaving Miranda to face the dragon alone. Upon returning to the inn, Miranda is told by her father
that she is to marry the barber. She refuses and
marries a member of a traveling troupe instead.

56   *Hann, Jacquie. Big Trouble. New York: Four
         Winds, 1978. grades K-3
While playing, two little girls create a monster
from clay. Mel, the clay creature, proceeds to
wreck the house. Refusing to share the blame for
the disorder, the girls argue about who has to take
Mel home with them. When the father asks about
the trouble, the girls quickly find their own solution
to their disagreement and are friends once more.

57   *Hapgood, Miranda. Martha's Mad Day. New York:
         Crown, 1977. grades Preschool-2
Martha wakes up one morning big, fierce, and mean
and continues acting mad all day.

58   *Hart, Carole. Delilah. New York: Harper &
         Row, 1973. grades 2-6
Ten-year-old Delilah likes to play basketball and
drums. An only child, Delilah is energetic and
enjoys people. Although she is not always happy,
Delilah makes the best of every situation, whether
it's receiving a dog instead of a record player for
her birthday or having her grandmother stay with her
when her parents are gone.

59   *Heller, Linda. Lily at the Table. New York:
         Macmillan, 1979. grades Preschool-2
Lily, who dislikes eating the food on her plate,
fantasizes about what she could do with the food.

60   **Hill, Donna. <u>Ms Glee Was Waiting.</u> New York:
      Atheneum, 1978. grades K-4
      Laura is late for her piano lesson. She tries all
      forms of transportation to get there, but something
      goes wrong with all of them--so she says!

61   *Himler, Ronald. <u>The Girl on the Yellow Giraffe.</u>
      New York: Harper & Row, 1976. grades
      Preschool-2
      A little girl sees the people, activities, and build-
      ings of the city in a more imaginative way.

62   *Hirsh, Marilyn. <u>The Secret Dinosaur.</u> New York:
      Holiday House, 1979. grades 1-4
      Jane and Bill discover the perfect spot for their
      picnic--a rock in the middle of the lake that turns
      out to be a dinosaur. In order to keep the dinosaur
      a secret, Jane and Bill find a way to earn money
      for the dinosaur's peanut-butter sandwiches and make
      daily trips to the lake to feed him--their very own
      secret dinosaur.

63   **Hoban, Russell. <u>Best Friends for Frances.</u> New
      York: Harper & Row, 1969. grades Pre-
      school-3
      Frances, a badger, convinces Albert of the value of
      friendship--not just for eating, but also for playing
      baseball, catching frogs and snakes, and having fun.
      This is one of a series of books about the young
      badgers.

64   Horvath, Betty. <u>Be Nice to Josephine.</u> New York:
      Watts, 1970. grades 1-4
      Charlie always plays baseball with his friends on
      Saturday. However, this Saturday, Charlie has to
      entertain his cousin Josephine. He plans a picnic
      and fishing. When she arrives, he makes her carry
      the fishing tackle, dig the worms, and eat the pea-
      nut-butter-and-mustard sandwich, but she doesn't
      complain. In fact, she volunteers. They fish, but
      Josephine doesn't mind baiting her hook. Charlie
      decides it really isn't too bad having to spend the
      day with a girl.

65   Hurwitz, Johanna. <u>Busybody Nora.</u> New York:
      Morrow, 1976. grades 1-5
      Five-year-old Nora wants to know everyone in her

apartment building. When her little brother decides
to have stone soup, the project involves several
other people and gives Nora the idea for achieving
her wish to have a building party.

66   *Jensen, Virginia Allen. Sara and the Door. Read-
      ing, Mass.: Addison-Wesley, 1977. grades
      K-1
Little Sara has a problem: her coat is stuck in
the door. Sara attempts several solutions and
finally succeeds--all by herself.

67   Jeschke, Susan. Victoria's Adventure. New York:
      Holt, Rinehart & Winston, 1976. grades
      Preschool-1
When Victoria is sick, she imagines that she visits
the North Pole and Jamaica with her toy bear and
doll.

68   *Johnston, Johanna. Supposings. New York: Holi-
      day House, 1967. grades Preschool-2
A little girl pretends that things can be any size
she chooses. She decides to be small enough to
slip through a spiderweb and enter the jungle of
flowers, where she meets various animals. Upon
seeing a huge bee, she decides to return to the
world where things are the "sizes they are natu-
rally."

69   Keats, Ezra Jack. Maggie and the Pirate. New
      York: Four Winds, 1979. grades K-3
Maggie's pet cricket is stolen by a "pirate" while
she is shopping for her mother. Concerned for
her cricket, Maggie tracks the thief. In the struggle
with the "pirate," the cricket is killed. Not in-
tending to have hurt the cricket, the "pirate" returns Maggie's cage with a new cricket inside, and
they find that they can be friends.

70   Keith, Eros. Nancy's Backyard. New York:
      Harper & Row, 1973. grades Preschool-3
While it is raining, four children tell of dreams
they have had. After the rain stops, the children
act out their dreams.

71   *Kellogg, Steven. Won't Somebody Play with Me?
      New York: Dial, 1972. grades Preschool-3

On her birthday, Kim finds that Timmy, Annie, and
Philip won't play with her. She imagines some terrible punishments for them. Later, when she discovers that they are having a surprise party for
her, she forgets all about being angry.

72   *Kingman, Lee. Georgina and the Dragon. Boston:
          Houghton Mifflin, 1972. grades 2-5
      Named after her great-grandmother, who helped get
      women the right to vote in Idaho, Georgina inherited
      not only her name but her determination as well.
      In attempting to earn some money for a trip,
      Georgina finds that males have all the opportunities.
      When Georgina discovers that three males dislike
      their jobs because of one person, Mrs. Livermore
      the Dragon, she decides to find out about her.
      Using diplomacy, Georgina discovers that Mrs.
      Livermore is lonely. Georgina's efforts to change
      people's attitudes and stereotypes earn her a re-
      porter's assignment, initiate a new business in-
      volving former competitiors, and stress the impor-
      tance of people needing each other.

73   Klein, Norma. Blue Trees, Red Sky. New York:
          Pantheon, 1975. grades 2-5
      Valerie's mother works as an artist, but Valerie
      wishes her mother didn't have to work so they could
      spend more time together. When Valerie's mother
      explains that she likes to work, Valerie understands
      that her mother loves her regardless of her working.

74   *Klein, Norma. Girls Can Be Anything. New York:
          Dutton, 1973. grades Preschool-1
      Marina and Adam are best friends in kindergarten.
      When they play, Adam thinks that he should be the
      doctor, pilot, and President. But, Marina feels
      that she should be able to play these same roles if
      she wants. After discussions with their parents,
      they find that they can both be satisfied through
      cooperation.

75   **Klein, Norma. A Train for Jane. New York:
          Feminist Press, 1974. grades K-4
      Jane's only Christmas wish is for a train. Although
      everyone in her family tries to talk her out of it
      and steer her toward more "feminine" toys, Jane
      remains adamant in wanting a train--and receives
      one.

76   Krasilovsky, Phyllis. The Girl Who Was a Cowboy.
      Garden City, N.Y.: Doubleday, 1965. grades
      Preschool-2
      Margaret enjoys playing cowboy with Michael. How-
      ever, when she leaves her hat at her grandmother's
      house, she doesn't feel like a cowboy anymore. Her
      grandmother sends her a cowboy hat along with another
      hat, and Margaret decides that she can dress as a
      cowboy and as a girl.

77   *La Farge, Phyllis. Granny's Fish Story. New York:
      Parents' Magazine, 1975. grades K-3
      Julie's grandmother wears sneakers and blue jeans
      and lives alone in the country. When Julie invites
      a friend to come with her to visit her grandmother,
      they hear about swamp halibut and bush mackerel;
      catch tadpoles, frogs, snakes, and turtles; climb
      trees; and build a small dam.

78   *La Farge, Phyllis. Joanna Runs Away. New York:
      Holt, Rinehart & Winston, 1973. grades K-4
      Joanna loves animals and looks forward to seeing
      Costanza, a horse who pulls the vegetable wagon
      around her Brooklyn neighborhood. She dreams of
      being with Costanza in a green field. Wanting to
      make her wish come true, Joanna hides in the back
      of the wagon and goes home with Costanza. After
      her attempt to escape with the horse is stopped,
      she discovers that she has been selfish both in
      wanting to take Costanza and in thinking that she
      was the only person to feel loneliness.

79   **Langner, Nola. Rafiki. New York: Viking, 1977.
      grades K-3
      On her way to build a treehouse, a little girl finds
      some animals in the jungle who need their houses
      cleaned. The lion, King of the Beasts, has told
      the animals that little girls, not animals, should
      clean houses. While the animals show Rafiki the
      jobs that need to be done, they find that they are
      able to do the jobs and, in fact, enjoy doing them.
      The lion agrees that the animals may do the house-
      work while the little girl builds her house.

80   *Lasker, Joe. Mothers Can Do Anything. Chicago:
      Whitman, 1972. grades K-3
      The text and illustrations show mothers in both

traditional and nontraditional roles--plumber, principal, dentist, telephone repair, cook, dancer, and
many others.

81   Lasker, Joe. The Strange Voyage of Neptune's
         Car. New York: Viking, 1977. grades K-4
      Captain Joshua Patten and his wife, Mary, embark
      upon a voyage around the Horn from New York to
      San Francisco in a race with two other ships. Dur-
      ing the voyage, the first mate disobeys the captain,
      Joshua becomes so ill he cannot see or hear, and
      the second mate doesn't know how to navigate. They
      discover that Mary is the only one aboard who is
      capable of commanding the ship. The story is
      based on a true event that occurred on November
      15, 1856.

82   *Lasky, Kathryn. My Island Grandma. New York:
         Warne, 1979. grades Preschool-3
      Abbey describes the summers she spends with her
      grandmother on an island, where they swim, pick
      berries, tell stories, explore, bake cookies, star
      gaze, and sail. Although they return to the city
      for the winter, Abbey remembers her grandmother
      as her "Island Grandma."

83   *Laurence, Ester Hauser. We're Off to Catch a
         Dragon. Nashville, Tenn.: Abingdon, 1969.
         grades K-2
      A group of children set out with their wagon to
      catch a dragon. They capture their dragon and
      decide that since one dragon is so much fun they
      want another one. After trapping another dragon,
      the children find that they receive more than they
      expected--lots of baby dragons.

84   *Leiner, Katherine. Ask Me What My Mother Does.
         New York: Watts, 1978. grades 1-5
      The book describes mostly nontraditional occupations
      --steeplejill, photographer, carpenter, musician,
      police officer, and judge--in which women are
      illustrated. The fact that the women are also
      mothers is emphasized.

85   Levy, Elizabeth. Lizzie Lies a Lot. New York:
         Delacorte, 1976. grades 2-5
      Nine-year-old Lizzie finds that her habitual lying

gets her into trouble, especially in relationships with her friends and family. However, Lizzie learns the hard way that people never trust a liar and makes efforts to reform.

86   *Levy, Elizabeth. Nice Little Girls. New York:
        Delacorte, 1974. grades 1-4
        When Jackie moves to a new school, she is expected to act like a "nice little girl." To the teacher, this means that she can't run the film projector or use tools to build a box, so Jackie decides to be a boy. She discovers that she can't be a boy, but elects to act like a boy instead. However, when Jackie acknowledges the fact that she is a girl who wants to build boxes, she discovers that there are others who feel the same. She gains a friend, and soon the entire class is involved in a project.

87   **Levy, Elizabeth. Something Queer Is Going On (A
        Mystery). New York: Delacorte, 1973.
        grades 1-4
        When Jill's dog disappears, she and Gwen search for him until they discover something suspicious about a neighbor's story. With the help of Jill's mother, they solve the mystery. Something Queer at the Ball Park: A Mystery; Something Queer at the Library (a mystery); and Something Queer on Vacation (a mystery) are sequels.

88   Lindgren, Astrid. Of Course Polly Can Do Almost
        Everything. Chicago: Follett, 1977. grades
        Preschool-3
        Little Polly boasts of her ability to be able to do anything. When their father is unable to find a Christmas tree, Polly's brother challenges her to find one since she said she could do almost everything. Polly succeeds in her endeavor. This book is a sequel to Of Course Polly Can Ride a Bike.

89   *Lisker, Sonia O. I Am. New York: Hastings
        House, 1973. grades 1-5
        A sister and brother play a game of careers in which they cooperate and complement each other. They are dancers, construction workers, doctors, clowns, detectives, and astronauts.

90   Lloyd, Norris. Katie and the Catastrophe. Chicago:

Reilly & Lee, 1968. grades 3-5
Katie, an eight-year-old living in South Carolina in
1920, dreams of catastrophes, although she has
little chance of ever being in one. During a routine
summer visit to an aunt in another town, Katie
finally has her opportunity (although it is a small
catastrophe) when a cloudburst causes a small flash
flood. Although her aunt is the heroine, Katie is a
little proud that she did not cry.

91   Lyles, Vina. The Spooky Hand Mystery. Chicago:
           Childrens Press, 1973. grades 1-4
Wally, Toby Ho, and Pom Pom look for a mystery
to solve at the Oceanside Summer Fair. As things
begin disappearing at the fair, the only clue seems
to be a spooky hand. However, when the hand
leaves a string of pink gum for the private eyes to
follow, they solve the mystery.

92   **McClenathan, Louise. My Mother Sends Her Wis-
           dom. New York: Morrow, 1979. grades
           Preschool-3
In fifteenth-century Russia, when the moneylender
comes to collect a debt, Katya's mother pays him
on successive months with a goose and a gander, two
pigs, and a sack of wheat. Each time, Katya re-
peats a riddle and says that her mother sends her
wisdom. At the end of three months, Katya's
mother considers the debt paid. The moneylender
claims she still owes money, but the judge considers
the price of the wisdom to be more than enough
compensation for the debt.

93   *Maestro, Betsy. In My Boat. New York: Crowell,
           1976. grades Preschool-1
As a little girl is sailing, she meets many animals,
but they don't have time to stop. However, when
her father arrives, he does stop to play with her.

94   **Mahy, Margaret. Ultra-Violet Catastrophe. New
           York: Parents' Magazine, 1975. grades K-3
When Sally has to stop being Horrible Stumper, the
tree pirate, to get cleaned up for a visit to her
aunt, she isn't very pleased. At her Aunt Anne's
house, Sally meets Great-uncle Magnus Pringle.
Sent off for a walk, Sally and Great-uncle Pringle
soon discover that they have much in common and

can enjoy their visit together.

95 *Marshall, James. <u>George and Martha</u> series.
Boston: Houghton Mifflin, 1972-78. grades
K-3
In this series of four books, including <u>George and</u>
<u>Martha Encore, George and Martha One Fine Day,</u>
and <u>George and Martha Rise and Shine</u>, George and
Martha are hippopotami who are friends. Each
book contains five mini-stories dealing with friend-
ship.

96 **Mayer, Marianna and Mercer. <u>Me and My Flying</u>
<u>Machine</u>. New York: Parents' Magazine,
1971. grades K-3
A child finds some old boards and nails, decides
to build a flying machine, and dreams of things to
do with it.

97 **Mayer, Mercer. <u>The Queen Always Wanted to</u>
<u>Dance.</u> New York: Simon & Schuster, 1971.
grades Preschool-3
Although it is unqueenly, the queen likes to dance
and sing. Embarrassed by her behavior, the king
signs laws forbidding singing and dancing in his
kingdom. Everyone obeys these laws for a time.
However, people miss having fun and begin breaking
the laws.

98 **Mayer, Mercer. <u>What Do You Do with a Kangaroo?</u>
New York: Four Winds, 1973. grades K-3
A little girl decides what to do with a kangaroo in
her bed, a possum in the bathroom, a llama in her
jeans, and several other animals.

99 *Merriam, Eve. <u>Boys & Girls, Girls & Boys.</u> New
York: Holt, Rinehart & Winston, 1972. grades
Preschool-3
Without stereotyping, this book lists a few of the
many activities and careers available to any child,
such as: helping with dishes, using imagination,
or being lion tamers.

100 *Merriam, Eve. <u>Mommies at Work</u>. New York:
Knopf, 1955. grades Preschool-2
The book shows some of the things that working
mothers do at home as well as on the job. It

lists both traditional and nontraditional roles and
shows that the child is not forgotten in these roles.

101 *Moncure, Jane Belk. Barbara's Pony, Buttercup.
      Chicago: Child's World, 1977. grades
      Preschool-3
      When Barbara rides her pony, she imagines all kinds
      of adventures--being an Indian princess, hunter,
      and acrobat. Even after Buttercup is hurt and
      becomes lame, Barbara discovers that Buttercup
      can pull a light pony cart, and they continue their
      adventures of being a pioneer and Cinderella.

102 **Ms. Foundation, Inc. Free to Be... You and Me.
      New York: McGraw-Hill, 1974. all ages
      This book contains a collection of songs, poems,
      and short stories that allow children to be who they
      are and what they can be.

103 **Nash, Ogden. The Adventures of Isabel. Boston:
      Little, Brown, 1963. grades 2-5
      Isabel meets a bear, a witch, a giant, a doctor,
      and monsters, but she is unafraid and calmly takes
      care of them without a fuss.

104 *Ness, Evaline, ed. and illus. Amelia Mixed the
      Mustard and Other Poems. New York:
      Scribner, 1975. grades 1-5
      Twenty poems of independent, nontraditional girls
      are presented.

105 *Ness, Evaline. Do You Have the Time, Lydia?
      New York: Dutton, 1971. grades K-3
      Lydia is so busy painting, reading, hammering,
      gathering, sewing, and baking that she never finishes
      anything. Her father, a florist, says that "if you
      take time you have time," but Lydia continues with
      her various activities. One day, her younger
      brother wants her to create a racing car for him
      from a lobster trap. She procrastinates and learns
      the importance of her father's statement.

106 Nicklaus, Carol. Katy Rose Is Mad. New York:
      Platt & Munk, 1975. grades Preschool-3
      Katy Rose is mad because she has to clean up her
      room before she can go outside to play baseball.
      She pulls towels on the floor, pushes dishes into the

sink, and pulls out her mother's flowers, but each
of these activities has a positive consequence.

107   Numeroff, Laura Joffe. Amy for Short. New York:
        Macmillan, 1976. grades 1-3
        As best friends, Amy and Mark do things together.
        When Amy grows to be taller than Mark, she begins
        to wonder whether they will still be best friends.
        For her birthday party, Amy invites her friends.
        However, Mark says that he cannot attend, and Amy
        is very upset. But, when a package arrives on her
        step, the day looks much brighter for Amy.

108   *Numeroff, Laura Joffe, and Richter, Alice Numeroff.
        Emily's Bunch. New York: Macmillan, 1978.
        grades K-3
        In planning her costume for a Halloween party, Emily
        has several ideas, but none of them satisfy her.
        Finally, Emily finds a very original costume idea
        that includes her friends--they dress in purple and
        become a bunch of grapes.

109   *Oppenheim, Joanne. Mrs. Peloki's Snake. New
        York: Dodd, Mead, 1980. grades 1-4
        When one of the boys reports a snake in the boys'
        bathroom, there is quite a stir in the second-grade
        classroom. Reluctantly, Mrs. Peloki enters the
        bathroom to confirm the report. While Mrs. Peloki
        is attempting to restore order to the classroom and
        get help, Stephanie decides to take action. She
        enters the bathroom, retrieves the snake, and re-
        veals its identity--"a fat gray string from a dirty
        old mop."

110   Oxenbury, Helen. The Queen and Rosie Randall.
        New York: Morrow, 1979. grades K-3
        The Queen calls on Rosie for the King's entertain-
        ment. Rosie suggests playing games like Blind-
        man's Bluff and Hide and Seek, which thoroughly
        satisfy the king and ambassadors.

111   *Paterson, Diane. Wretched Rachel. New York:
        Dial, 1978. grades Preschool-2
        Sometimes, Rachel does very good things. At
        other times, she does perfectly wretched things.
        But, during all these times, she is still loved.

112 *Pearson, Susan. <u>Monnie Hates Lydia</u>. New York:
      Dial, 1975. grades 2-4
      Monnie is excited over her big sister Lydia's tenth
      birthday party and helps her father with the special
      preparations. When her birthday arrives, Lydia is
      very grouchy, and Monnie can't seem to do anything
      to please her. As the day continues, things get
      worse. Then, Monnie is able to get even with Lydia
      in a very surprising and satisfying way.

113 *Porter, Wesley. <u>Kat Shelley and the Midnight Ex-
      press</u>. New York: Westport Communications
      Group, 1979. grades 2-5
      During a flood, a train engine falls into the river
      when the bridge is washed out. Kate runs a mile
      and a quarter through the rain to reach the nearest
      station so the next train will not be wrecked. This
      is based on a true story.

114 Quackenbush, Robert. <u>Sheriff Sally Gopher and the
      Haunted Dance Hall</u>. New York: Lothrop,
      Lee & Shepard, 1977. grades 1-4
      Sheriff Sally Gopher solves the mystery of the
      haunted dancehall in time for a performance by Lola
      Field Mouse, a famous dancer.

115 **Reavin, Sam. <u>Hurray For Captain Jane!</u> New York:
      Parents' Magazine, 1971. grades K-3
      Jane wins a bag of jellybeans, a waxed paper sailor's
      hat, and a bar of soap at a party. As she takes her
      bath wearing the hat and using the soap, she fantasizes
      that the water in the tub is the ocean, and she is the
      first woman captain of an ocean liner. A crisis
      occurs when an iceberg is sighted, but Captain Jane
      has the situation well in hand.

116 *Reed, Tom. <u>Melissa on Parade</u>. Scarsdale, N.Y.:
      Bradbury, 1979. grades K-2
      Melissa tries to be in every parade that comes to
      town, but she always seems to be in the way. One
      day, as she watches a parade instead of participating,
      she notices a bank robber trying to make his getaway.
      How she helps to capture the burglar achieves her
      dearest wish.

117 **Reesink, Marijke. <u>The Princess Who Always Ran
      Away</u>. New York: McGraw-Hill, 1981. grades
      K-4

The youngest daughter of a very strict king is very different from her sisters--she doesn't like wearing beautiful clothes, playing music, doing embroidery, or being closed up indoors. Whenever she gets the opportunity, she runs away until the soldiers return her to the castle, where she is punished. The king finally resorts to placing her in a huge ball in the sea to teach her a lesson, but a fisherman recovers the ball. The princess frees herself from the ball and escapes--never to be seen again.

118   *Robison, Nancy. The Lizard Hunt. New York: Lothrop, Lee & Shepard, 1979. grades 1-3 Talley wants to earn money by catching lizards. She takes her younger brother Greg along to provide the rope for the bag and to hold the bag of lizards they catch. While chasing a blue belly lizard, they get lost, but Greg is able to lead them out. Despite their ordeal, Talley manages to talk Greg into lizard hunting again if she searches and he rescues.

119   *Rockwell, Anne. The Girl with a Donkey Tail. New York: Dutton, 1979. grades 1-4 Cloralinda, a girl with a donkey tail, lives in a cave with three bears. One day just before spring, Cloralinda finds a gold ring with a message that says, "Take me to the princess." With this command, Cloralinda sets out and braves the animals of a strange forest, a hedge of thorns, and a swirling river to return the ring. Using the advice of others and some magic, Cloralinda discovers that she is the lost princess.

120   **Rosen, Winifred. Henrietta, the Wild Woman of Borneo. New York: Four Winds, 1975. grades K-3 With her bushy hair and "wild" behavior, Henrietta is called the Wild Woman of Borneo. To get away from her family (especially her critical older sister), Henrietta decides to mail herself to Borneo and enlists the willing aid of her sister. However, before Henrietta gets "mailed," her parents (with her sister's help) intervene and convince her that she is just what they want. Henrietta and the Day of the Iguana and Henrietta and the Gong from Hong Kong are sequels.

121   Ross, Jessica. Ms. Klondike. New York: Viking,
            1977. grades Preschool-2
        Ms. Klondike thinks she has finally found a job she
        is good at and that she likes--a taxicab driver.
        However, people start making comments about
        women drivers, and she is ready to quit her job.
        But, when an emergency arises, Ms. Klondike does
        some quick thinking to save the situation and her
        job.

122   *Rothman, Joel. I Can Be Anything You Can Be!
            New York: Scroll, 1973. grades K-4
        A little boy names typically male professions, but
        the little girl insists that she can also join those
        professions.

123   *St. George, Judith. By George, Bloomers! New
            York: Coward, McCann & Geoghegan, 1976.
            grades K-6
        In 1852, eight-year-old Hannah wants to wear
        bloomers so she can run, skate, and climb without
        worrying about her skirt. However, her mother
        says bloomers aren't ladylike. While climbing one
        day, Hannah accidentally rips her dress and makes
        herself some bloomers to wear. Hannah finally
        wins her mother's approval of bloomers when, in
        her bloomers, she rescues her little brother from
        a roof.

124   *St. George, Judith. The Halloween Pumpkin Smasher.
            New York: Putnam, 1978. grades 2-4
        Pumpkins are being smashed every night. Mary
        Grace and her imaginary friend Nellie want to dis-
        cover the culprit before their pumpkin is smashed.
        As they track several suspects, Mary Grace elimi-
        nates them as she discovers the facts and reveals
        the real culprit. She also discovers that she can be
        smart, brave, and kind.

125   *Saito, Michiko. Jenny's Journey. New York:
            McGraw-Hill, 1974. grades Preschool-3
        With her cat, Jenny sets out for a hike in the woods,
        where she encounters rabbits that invite them to the
        Flower Garden, bears that give a rock concert, and
        birds that need their help in rescuing baby birds.

126   **Schlein, Miriam. The Girl Who Would Rather

Climb Trees. New York: Harcourt Brace
Jovanovich, 1975. grades Preschool-3
Melissa is a lot of different people--a bird-watcher,
roller-skater, cook, reader, and tree-climber. But,
one thing she doesn't do is play with dolls. When
she is given a doll, Melissa manages to find a way
to play with her doll to please the adults and to
climb trees to please herself.

127   *Schulman, Janet. Jenny and the Tennis Nut. New
        York: Greenwillow, 1978. grades 1-4
Jenny's father wants to teach her to play tennis, but
Jenny prefers gymnastics. After trying to help her
several times, her father decides that gymnastics
is really Jenny's game and promises to get her
some equipment.

128   **Shecter, Ben. Hester the Jester. New York:
        Harper & Row, 1977. grades 1-3
Hester wants to be a jester like her father, but
girls can't be jesters. When Hester's father cannot
make the king laugh, Hester is given the opportunity
and succeeds. Then, Hester is allowed to be a
knight and a king.

129   Shulevitz, Uri. Rain Rain Rivers. New York:
        Farrar, Straus & Giroux, 1969. grades K-3
Inside her house, a girl thinks about the rain, from
its falling on her window to its raining over the
ocean. She looks forward to the next day when she
can walk barefoot in the mud and sail boats in the
puddles.

130   *Singer, Marilyn. The Pickle Plan. New York:
        Dutton, 1978. grades 1-3
Rachel is curious about a lot of things, but no one
seems to care or be interested in her. After attempting to make friends using three plans, Rachel
tries the direct approach. She asks a boy why he
always has a pickle in his lunch and finds that they
have a lot in common.

131   *Smith, Lucia B. My Mom Got a Job. New York:
        Holt, Rinehart & Winston, 1979. grades K-3
A little girl tells how things have changed since her
mother got a job. She relates the things she misses,
but also states the things that are better.

132 **Stevenson, Drew. <u>The Ballad of Penelope Lou ...</u>
<u>and Me.</u> Trumansburg, N.Y.: Crossing
Press, 1978. grades 1-4
Living in the late 1800s, Penelope Lou sails a ship
alone all over the world. When she returns to the
New England coast to settle down, Penelope Lou
states that she wants a man with courage to match
her own and someone able to face Davy Jones.
Although afraid of water, a young man finds a way
to marry Penelope Lou. However, after they are
married, Penelope Lou discovers the truth, but she
casually proclaims that they "have much to learn
from each other."

133 *Taylor, Mark. <u>Jennie Jenkins.</u> Boston: Little,
Brown, 1975. all ages
Jennie Jenkins is the only gal "who can plow and
hoe and help with hayin', dig 'taters, milk a cow,
chop wood, hitch a team, and ride Contraption!"
She sets out to spoil her three older sisters' chances
of getting married, but her plans backfire.

134 **Thayer, Jane. <u>Quiet on Account of Dinosaur.</u> New
York: Morrow, 1964. grades K-3
Being very knowledgeable on the subject of dinosaurs,
Mary Ann is delighted to discover the last dinosaur
in the world. She takes him to school, where everyone enjoys him until word of his presence reaches
others. The noises scare the dinosaur until the
children find a solution. When she grows up, Mary
Ann becomes <u>the</u> expert on dinosaurs.

135 *Torgersen, Don Arthur. <u>The Girl Who Tricked the</u>
<u>Troll.</u> Chicago: Childrens Press, 1978.
grades K-4
Karin picks troll berries, which causes a troll to
appear. Quickly becoming a nuisance on the farm,
the troll promises never to leave unless Karin can
ask him a question he cannot answer. After several
tries, Karin succeeds.

136 *Udry, Janice May. <u>Angie.</u> New York: Harper &
Row, 1971. grades 1-5
Angie has a goose for a pet, goes into a haunted
house alone, makes friends with the principal, discovers a way to make money to buy a birthday present, fixes an "antique" shoeshine chair, and has a

terrific imagination for creative-writing assignments.

137 *Van Woerkom, Dorothy. Becky and the Bear. New
York: Putnam, 1975. grades 1-4
Eight-year-old Becky watches as her father and
older brother go to hunt for fresh meat. She wishes
that she could go hunting and be brave, but her
grandmother tells her to stir the pudding. Becky
gets her chance to be brave and intelligent when a
bear approaches the cabin where Becky is alone.

138 **Van Woerkom, Dorothy. The Queen Who Couldn't
Bake Gingerbread. New York: Knopf, 1975.
grades Preschool-3
The King decides he needs a wife. His Queen must
be wise, beautiful, and able to bake gingerbread.
He finally finds a Princess who is wise but not so
beautiful and she can't bake gingerbread. However,
she also has some qualifications for her husband.
He must be as kind as he is handsome and be able
to play the slide trombone. They finally are able
to reach a compromise and marry. But one day,
the King mistakenly mentions gingerbread, and the
Queen says slide trombone. This begins a disagreement that they are able to resolve creatively.

139 **Viorst, Judith. Rosie and Michael. New York:
Atheneum, 1978. grades 1-4
Two children, Rosie and Michael, discover what
it takes to be friends--acceptance, sharing, understanding, and support.

140 Wahl, Jan. A Wolf of My Own. New York: Macmillan, 1969. grades K-2
For her birthday, a little girl receives a wolf puppy
and imagines the things they will do together.

141 **Wells, Rosemary. Benjamin and Tulip. New York:
Dial, 1973. grades Preschool-2
Benjamin and Tulip are raccoons. Benjamin has
problems with Tulip when she keeps beating him up.
He also gets scolded from his aunt for bothering
"that sweet little girl." In the end, Benjamin and
Tulip find a way that they can be equals and friends.

142 *Wells, Rosemary. Noisy Nora. New York: Dial,
1973. grades Preschool-2

A little-girl mouse feels neglected by her family
and makes noise to get their attention. However,
when Nora runs away, the house becomes too quiet,
and everyone becomes concerned. Her family is
relieved when Nora comes crashing home.

143 *Wells, Rosemary. Unfortunately Harriet. New
York: Dial, 1972. grades Preschool-3
When Harriet spills varnish on a new brown rug,
she tries several ways to remove the stain before
her mother sees it. Nothing is successful, and
she considers running away. But, just in time, the
new rug arrives to be placed over the brown padding.

144 **Werth, Kurt, and Watts, Mabel. Molly and the Giant.
New York: Parents' Magazine, 1973. grades
K-3
Unable to support his three daughters, a father
sends them to seek their fortunes. Being beautiful,
brave, and smart, the youngest of the sisters, Molly,
leads them to a giant's house hidden in the woods.
Through bravery and cleverness, Molly is able to
retrieve stolen goods from the giant and acquire
husbands for herself and her sisters.

145 **Wiesner, William. Turnabout. New York: Seabury, 1972. grades Preschool-3
A farmer thinks his wife's work is easier than his,
so they agree to change jobs for a day. The wife
goes out to work in the fields while the husband
stays to do the housework. Before the day is over,
the husband finds that his wife's work is harder
than he anticipated and willingly returns to the fields.

146 **Williams, Barbara. Kevin's Grandma. New York:
Dutton, 1975. grades K-3
Kevin and a friend contrast their grandmothers'
activities, dress, and lifestyles--when the boys are
sick, one grandmother brings presents and ice
cream while Kevin's grandmother brings him Mad
magazine and peanut-butter soup. Kevin's grandmother does many other "un-grandmotherly" things
--according to Kevin.

147 **Williams, Jay. Petronella. New York: Parents'
Magazine, 1973. grades K-3
The third child in a family with two brothers,

Petronella sets out to seek her fortune. Determined
to find her prince even if she has to rescue him
herself, Petronella succeeds at three tasks to free
the prince from the enchanter.

148   **Williams, Jay.   The Practical Princess.   New York:
          Parents' Magazine, 1969.   grades K-3
       When Bedelia is born, she is given beauty, grace,
       and common sense by three fairies.   As she matures,
       she finds it necessary to use these qualities when
       a dragon demands a princess to eat and a ruler
       demands her for his wife.   She decides that she
       must rescue herself.

149   **Williams, Jay.   The Question Box.   New York:
          Norton, 1965.   grades K-3
       In the fourteenth century, Maria is always asking
       questions about how and why things work the way
       they do.   People tease her and call her a question
       box.   On her eighth birthday, Maria asks her father
       how the Great Clock works, but he has to admit
       that he doesn't know.   Not being satisfied, Maria
       discovers for herself how the clock works and is
       able to save the town from an invading army using
       this knowledge.

150   *Yolen, Jane.   The Girl Who Loved the Wind.   New
          York: Crowell, 1972.   grades K-3
       In order to avoid unhappiness, Danina's father
       locks her in a palace surrounded on three sides
       by high walls and the sea on the fourth.   However,
       for all his effort, he cannot keep the wind and its
       song outside.   When the wind enters, it tells Danina
       of a different, changing, and challenging world.   As
       she wonders about the outside world, the palace
       becomes her prison, and she escapes to discover the
       world for herself.

151   *Young, Merriam.   If I Rode a Dinosaur.   New York:
          Lothrop, Lee & Shepard, 1974.   grades K-3
       Visiting a museum, a little girl imagines the wonder-
       ful adventures she could have if she were able to
       ride different dinosaurs.

152   *Young, Merriam.   Jellybeans for Breakfast.   New
          York: Parents' Magazine, 1968.   grades K-3
       Two little girls imagine all the things they can do with
       jellybeans.

153   **Young, Merriam. <u>So What If It's Raining!</u> New York:
          Parents' Magazine, 1976.   grades Preschool-3
          On a rainy day, a girl and boy imagine themselves
          as rescuers, gunfighters, circus clowns, cowboys,
          elves, and scientists.

154   Zimmerman, Andrea Griffing. <u>Yetta the Trickster.</u>
          New York: Seabury, 1978.   grades 1-4
          Yetta enjoys playing tricks on everyone. Even
          when her tricks backfire, she is able to laugh at
          herself, but she continues to play tricks just the
          same.

155   Zolotow, Charlotte. <u>When I Have a Little Girl.</u>
          New York: Harper & Row, 1965.   grades K-
          2
          A little girl thinks about raising a little girl when
          all the rules would be different--she would be
          allowed to do all the things she is not allowed to do
          now.

GENERAL
FICTION, INTERMEDIATE

---

156 **Aiken, Joan. The Cuckoo Tree. Garden City,
N. Y.: Doubleday, 1971. grades 4-7
Picked up by a ship off the coast of Nantucket,
Dido Twite accompanies the wounded captain to
deliver an urgent, secret dispatch to London in
1848, when their coach overturns. While the
captain recuperates, Dido must find a way to get
the dispatch to London. She also becomes in-
creasingly curious about a cuckoo tree and its
significance, a boy and his strange grandmother
who seeks to keep him isolated, another "boy" who
must live in an old attic without being seen, and
two old women who meet secretly for suspicious
purposes. This is a sequel to Nightbirds on Nantucket.

157 **Aiken, Joan. Nightbirds on Nantucket. New York:
Dell, 1969. grades 4-7
Having been rescued at sea by a passing ship, Dido
is given boy's clothes, a haircut, and the task of
attempting to get the captain's daughter (Dutiful
Penitence) to come out of a locked closet. With
patience and intelligence, Dido succeeds in bolstering
Dutiful Penitence's courage a little. The girls are
left in Nantucket with Dutiful's Aunt Tribulation to
care for them. However, puzzles abound as Aunt
Trib behaves strangely and mysterious men make
frightening plans, but Dido is adventurous enough to
discover the solution. This is the sequel to Black
Hearts in Battersea, which follows The Wolves of
Willoughby Chase.

33

158 **Aiken, Joan. <u>The Wolves of Willoughby Chase</u>.
       New York: Dell, 1962. grades 4-7
       Expecting her young cousin Sylvia, Bonnie rushes
       down the staircase and falls headlong at the feet of
       her new governess, Miss Slighcarp. Miss Slighcarp
       sternly and coldly surveys her young, active charge
       and decides that lessons on deportment will take
       priority. Just after Bonnie's parents leave on a
       trip, Bonnie and Sylvia begin to be suspicious of
       their governess when she locks Bonnie in a closet
       for punishment, dismisses the servants, wears
       Bonnie's mother's best gowns, and begins burning
       important documents. Only Bonnie and Sylvia can
       do anything to stop Miss Slighcarp.

159 **Alexander, Lloyd. <u>The Wizard in the Tree</u>. New
       York: Dutton, 1975. grades 4-7
       When Mallory finds the wizard Arbican caught in a
       tree, she helps him out, and, believing in fairy
       tales, she hopes to be rewarded with three wishes.
       However, the wizard claims that magicians can't
       work miracles but only create illusions. Besides,
       Arbican finds that being trapped in the tree for so
       long has altered his powers, and they can't be
       relied upon. In order for him to return to the
       other magic folk in Vale Innis, he finds that he
       must depend on spunky Mallory to get him out of
       the predicaments he gets them into.

160 *Anderson, Mary. <u>Emma's Search for Something</u>.
       New York: Atheneum, 1973. grades 4-6
       Emma Pigeon (a real pigeon) had always been satis-
       fied with her roles of wife and mother, but one
       spring day, Emma begins to have a peculiar feeling.
       Her husband suggests a change of scenery, so she
       visits with some birds in Central Park. Still unable
       to satisfy her peculiar feeling, she uses her ability
       to read and visits the library. Upon learning about
       heritage, she attempts to help people by being a
       carrier pigeon. Her efforts change the family roles
       and routines to encourage mutual admiration, re-
       spect, and understanding.

161 *Anderson, Mary. <u>F. T. C. Superstar</u>. New York:
       Atheneum, 1976. grades 4-6
       After returning from his summer vacation, Freddie
       the Cat feels disgusted and depressed. Freddie

wants to return to New Jersey to watch actors perform in summer stock. Emma Pigeon helps Freddie
out of his doldrums by reading and teaching him to
become an actor. They spend weeks practicing and
polishing his talent for his stage debut. Finally,
with his typed résumé in mouth, Freddie appears at
a Broadway stage door for his audition. This is the
sequel to Emma's Search for Something.

162 Anderson, Mary. Matilda's Masterpiece. New York:
      Atheneum, 1977. grades 4-6
      Having solved several home and school mysteries,
      twelve-year-old Matilda (Mattie) thinks she is ready
      for some high-class crimes. Mattie sees her oppor-
      tunity on a class field trip to the Brooklyn Museum
      when a valuable painting is stolen and she knows the
      thief. She follows her instincts and with some luck
      is able to solve the crime.

163 **Babbitt, Natalie. Tuck Everlasting. New York:
      Farrar, Straus & Giroux, 1975. grades 4+
      An only child living in the West in the 1880s, ten-
      year-old Winnie wants to do something that will
      make some difference in the world. Going into the
      woods, where she has never been, Winnie discovers
      a boy drinking from a stream. Winnie is kidnapped
      so the Tuck family can explain to her the importance
      of keeping their secret--a drink from the stream
      brings immortality. When the Tuck family secret
      is in danger of being exposed by an evil stranger,
      Mrs. Tuck shoots him and is jailed. Winnie realizes
      the urgency of releasing Mrs. Tuck from jail and
      helps to plan and implement the successful escape.

164 *Balderson, Margaret. When Jays Fly to Barbmo.
      New York: World, 1969. grades 7+
      Living in Norway prior to World War II with her
      father and an aunt, fourteen-year-old Ingeborg has
      always been curious about her mother. However,
      her mother is never mentioned and she knows not
      to ask. After her father is killed and her aunt
      dies, Ingeborg knows that she wants to go with the
      Laplanders (her mother's family) to learn more
      about her mother and herself. However, she finds
      that she is not happy with a nomadic life and re-
      turns to her father's cabin.

165 **Barford, Carol. <u>Let Me Hear the Music</u>. New
        York: Seabury, 1979. grades 5-8
        After experiencing the tragic death of Bennie, her
        best friend, twelve-year-old Ryn asks herself and
        her Depression-haunted family whether life will
        always be so hard for them. Ryn's questions start
        her family acting independently and assertively in-
        stead of fearfully and passively.

166 *Bauer, Marion Dane. <u>Shelter from the Wind</u>. New
        York: Seabury, 1976. grades 5-12
        Feeling that she has been replaced by her new step-
        mother, twelve-year-old Stacey runs away from her
        only home across the dusty, dry Oklahoma panhandle.
        Having no real plan (except maybe to find her mother,
        who had deserted the family) and no supplies, Stacey
        spends a terrifying night on the desert. Two German
        shepherds lead her to their mistress. Old Ella,
        a fiercely independent and unsentimental woman,
        gives Stacey aid and helps her to face herself. When
        old Ella sprains her ankle and the female dog gives
        birth to pups, Stacey has to make some crucial
        decisions, which she discovers she is able to do.

167 Bawden, Nina. <u>Carrie's War.</u> Philadelphia:
        Lippincott, 1973. grades 4-7
        During World War II, twelve-year-old Carrie and
        her younger brother Nick are sent from their home
        in war-torn London to live in the safer Welsh
        countryside. They are selected to live with penny-
        pinching Mr. Evans and his sister. Life in the
        Evans household is difficult, but it is made more
        bearable by their visits to Druid's Bottom, where
        the Evanses' estranged sister lives with her house-
        keeper. During their visits, the children coax the
        housekeeper into telling about the skull and the curse
        that hangs over the house. When London is safe,
        the children return, but it isn't until many years
        later that Carrie is actually able to deal with the
        curse.

168 Bawden, Nina. <u>Rebel on a Rock</u>. Philadelphia:
        Lippincott, 1978. grades 5-9
        With her family, twelve-year-old Jo visits Ithaca,
        a country ruled by a dictator. She becomes involved
        with secrets of a revolution.

169   *Bawden, Nina. The Witch's Daughter. Philadelphia:
            Lippincott, 1966. grades 4-6
        Ten-year-old Perdita, known to the children of the
        village as a witch, does not go to school or associate
        with other children and is allowed to "run wild."
        When Janey, who is blind, and her brother Tim
        come to the island, they become friends with Perdita
        and find themselves involved in some jewel thieves'
        plan to escape.

170   **Beatty, John and Patricia. Master Rosalind. New
            York: Morrow, 1974. grades 7+
        Though of gentle birth, twelve-year-old Rosalind
        Broome refuses to be brought up with ladylike vir-
        tues. While delivering a book for her grandfather
        and dressed as a boy, she is kidnapped, taken to the
        rogues of London, and baptized as one of them.
        Failing to become a proper pickpocket, Rosalind is
        sent on her way. Since it is unlawful for a girl to
        be a player, Rosalind dresses as a boy so she may
        become a player in a traveling theater troupe.

171   Beatty, Patricia. By Crumbs, It's Mine! New
            York: Morrow, 1976. grades 5-9
        On her way to the Arizona Territory with her
        family in 1882, thirteen-year-old Damaris finds
        that she is the owner of a collapsible traveling
        hotel. Although her father leaves the train when
        the cry of gold is heard, the family continues to
        the Arizona Territory to make a living as hotel-
        keepers. Since her father does not return, Damaris
        sets out to bring him home. When she finds him,
        Damaris also finds the man who had given her the
        hotel, makes a deal with him, and assures the
        family of money to return to Missouri.

172   *Beatty, Patricia. How Many Miles to Sundown.
            New York: Morrow, 1974. grades 5-9
        Thirteen-year-old Beeler "ain't much for pretty,
        but she's surely active." When her eleven-year-
        old brother Leo leaves home and takes Beeler's
        horse, Beeler immediately follows him. She takes
        her critter (a longhorn steer named Travis) with
        her, as he makes an excellent watchdog. When
        Beeler is locked in a carrot cellar by her brother,
        she is forced to ride Travis, since Leo has taken
        her horse again. But she doesn't give up, and

"Beeler don't mind nobody unless she's got a mind
to." Their journey continues throughout the South-
west of the 1880s to help a friend locate his father.

173   *Beatty, Patricia.   Just Some Weeds from the Wilder-
            ness.   New York: Morrow, 1978.   grades
            7-9
       On New Year's Eve of 1873, Lucinda discovers that
       her aunt and uncle are "ruined"--money has been
       borrowed that cannot be repaid.   It appears that
       Lucinda, her brother, and widowed mother may have
       to return to other relatives in Tennessee.   By con-
       cocting a "wonder-working elixir," her Aunt Adelina
       attempts to recover the money needed to pay their
       debts.   However, this enterprise meets with the
       disapproval of her husband and several formula
       failures before a successful batch is discovered.
       The book is based on the life of Lydia Pinkham.

174   Beatty, Patricia.   The Lady from Black Hawk.
            New York: McGraw-Hill, 1967.   grades 4-6
       Living in a gold boom town in 1884, Julie resolves
       to get her father a wife.   Her main purpose is to
       have good food to eat and clean clothes ironed,
       since she isn't very good at these things.   Julie
       does the best she can to keep her brothers healthy
       (which even includes fighting the town bully with
       them), but things improve tremendously when Julie
       succeeds in her goal.

175   **Beatty, Patricia.   Something to Shout About.   New
            York: Morrow, 1976.   grades 5-9
       When the founding fathers of Ottenberg (a gold-
       mining town in Montana Territory) decide to build a
       new jail and city hall but merely to remodel a
       chicken coop for the school in 1875, they didn't
       plan on contending with the women of the town.
       The women seek to raise money for a new school
       by collecting donations in the town's thirty-eight
       saloons.   Thirteen-year-old Hope begins a protest
       against an uncooperative bar-owner by sitting out-
       side the saloon door and is soon joined by other
       women.   Their efforts to raise enough money for
       the schoolhouse are successful.

176   **Beatty, Patricia.   The Staffordshire Terror.   New
            York: Morrow, 1979.   grades 5-9

Thirteen-year-old Cissie finds a very young puppy
whose mother has been killed. While doing an
English assignment, she discovers that her dog is
a Staffordshire terrier, a breed of fighting dog.
Her uncle visits and shows considerable interest in
the terrier. When he leaves after a family quarrel,
Cissie's dog also disappears. Determined to get
the dog back, Cissie follows her uncle from dog-
fighting match to match.

177 **Beatty, Patricia. That's One Ornery Orphan.
New York: Morrow, 1980. grades 5-9
After her grandfather dies, thirteen-year-old Hallie
is forced to go to a Texas county orphanage in the
1870s. When it appears that she may be picked by
a farmer, Hallie invents stories about her family
background to discourage him. Hallie is placed with
three different foster families. However, when she
puts red pepper in the preacher's snuff, mixes up
several similar babies, mishandles a babysitting
assignment, and hires the town's old milkwagon
mare for a play, she is sent back to the orphanage.
The director arranges a placement for Hallie with
the farmer, where she learns that she is wanted
for a daughter not as a hired hand.

178 *Bellairs, John. The Figure in the Shadows. New
York: Dial, 1975. grades 7+
Lewis and Rose Rita (sixth-graders) perform a test
on an old coin to determine its magical powers.
Lewis discovers that it does have magical powers
but doesn't tell anyone until mysterious notes and
a dark figure appear to frighten him. Rose Rita
is needed to help solve the mystery.

179 **Bellairs, John. The Letter, the Witch, and the
Ring. New York: Dial, 1976. grades 7+
Rose Rita's best friend, Lewis, will be spending
the summer at boy-scout camp, so Rose Rita plans
on spending a boring summer alone at home. However, Mrs. Zimmerman, a witch, receives a strange
letter from an eccentric uncle who is leaving his
farm to Mrs. Zimmerman. She invites Rose Rita
on a vacation to visit the farm, and strange things
begin to happen. This is the sequel to The Figure
in the Shadows.

180   Blume, Judy. <u>Blubber</u>. Scarsdale, N.Y.: Brad-
        bury, 1974. grades 4-6
        Linda, a fifth-grade girl, is mercilessly teased by
        everyone in her class, but especially by four girls.
        When Jill suspects that the one girl who directs the
        teasing may have told about a Halloween prank, Jill
        suddenly becomes the victim of teasing also. Jill
        learns that she has to have a mind of her own in
        order to feel good about herself.

181   **Bolton, Carole. <u>Never Jam Today</u>. New York:
        Atheneum, 1971. grades 5-9
        Living in New York in 1917, seventeen-year-old
        Maddie becomes so upset with her father's "medi-
        eval thinking" that she volunteers to work for suf-
        frage. When he locks her out of the house and re-
        fuses to let her come home until she comes to her
        senses, she goes to live with her aunt. Maddie
        joins the more militant suffragists, walks the picket
        lines, and goes to prison, where she becomes even
        more adamant about the vote. When the Nineteenth
        Amendment is ratified, Maddie realizes that women's
        rights is a continuing struggle and decides to leave
        home to start her own life.

182   **Bradbury, Bianca. <u>"I'm Vinny, I'm Me."</u> Boston:
        Houghton Mifflin, 1977. grades 5-9
        After their mother dies, sixteen-year-old Vinny
        and her twelve-year-old brother discover that they
        must combine their skills, learn from each other,
        and find their individual identities in order to keep
        their motel running. The state welfare department
        wants to place them in separate foster homes.
        With their perseverance and cooperation and help
        from friends, Vinny and Tim are able to make a
        life for themselves.

183   *Bradbury, Bianca. <u>In Her Father's Footsteps</u>.
        Boston: Houghton Mifflin, 1976. grades 5-9
        Jenny had decided long ago that she would go to
        college, become a veterinarian, and go into partner-
        ship with her father. When a fire destroys her
        father's animal hospital, everything seems to go
        wrong. In addition to financial problems, her
        father begins to date a woman who seems to
        threaten Jenny's relationship with her father, and
        Jenny is concerned about a boy's new interest in

her. Jenny finds that there is a place for everything in her life--a stepmother, a boyfriend, her
father, as well as her feelings and ambitions.

184   Bradbury, Bianca. Mixed-Up Summer. Boston:
            Houghton Mifflin, 1979. grades 7+
        Gay must decide about a career, marriage, or both.

185   Bradbury, Bianca. Two on an Island. Boston:
            Houghton Mifflin, 1965. grades 4-6
        Jeff and Trudy, twelve and nine years old, want
        to surprise their grandmother by arriving for their
        visit a few days early. When she isn't home, they
        row over to an island to play and swim. The boat
        floats away, and Jeff and Trudy find themselves
        marooned within sight of the city, but unable to
        catch anyone's attention. During the three days
        before their rescue, they learn to depend on each
        other for support and find themselves becoming
        friends.

186   Branscum, Robbie. The Saving of P. S. Garden
            City, N. Y.: Doubleday, 1977. grades 5-7
        Priscilla Sue, the last child born in Preacher Blue's
        family, is called P. S. Her mother died just after
        P. S. was born, so she is left to care for her
        father. At twelve, she finds that her father is
        planning to marry a city woman with two daughters.
        P. S. is jealous, since she feels that she is best
        able to take care of and love her father. When
        she thinks that the family would be better off with-
        out her, P. S. runs away. Her brother brings her
        home, where she realizes that she has been selfish
        and resentful, and she decides to "change her ways."

187   *Bridgers, Sue Ellen. All Together Now. New York:
            Knopf, 1979. grades 7+
        Twelve-year-old Casey spends the summer with her
        grandparents in a small southern town while her
        father fights in the Korean War and her mother
        works two jobs. Through the companionship of a
        thirty-three-year-old retarded man, Casey finds the
        love of a family and discovers that love includes
        risks and demands the responsibility to do some-
        thing about it.

188   **Brink, Carol Ryrie. Caddie Woodlawn. New York:

Macmillan, 1935. grades 4-7
Eleven-year-old Caddie is brought up in a very
nontraditional way, especially for the 1860s. She
is allowed to run "as wild as a little tomboy" with
her two brothers. Carol Brink based Caddie Woodlawn on her grandmother's childhood as a Wisconsin
pioneer. Magical Melons is the sequel.

189   *Brink, Carol Ryrie. Louly. New York: Macmillan,
          1974. grades 4-7
"Louly was not afraid of being different. She did
what she longed to do as well as she could." In
fact, fifteen-year-old Louly cannot resist any challenge, including the responsibility for a younger
sister for six weeks while her parents are away.
However, her foremost goal is to win the silver
loving cup for her recitation at the county speech
contest. With practice and determination, Louly
achieves her goal.

190   *Brown, Palmer. Beyond the Pawpaw Trees. New
          York: Avon, 1954. grades 3-5
Anna Lavinia has never been beyond the pawpaw
trees--not for shopping, going to school, or playing.
One day, "a lavender blue day when special things
happen," Anna Lavinia's mother states that it is
time for Anna Lavinia to visit her father's sister.
So, for the first time in her life, Anna Lavinia goes
beyond the pawpaw trees, where adventure awaits
her--a desert, a Pasha, a camel, an island in the
sky, and her father.

191   **Bulla, Clyde Robert. Shoeshine Girl. New York:
          Crowell, 1975. grades 4-6
As a shoeshine girl, Sarah Ida learns the value of
money and responsibility when she keeps the shoeshine stand open while the owner is in the hospital.

192   **Burch, Robert. Ida Early Comes Over the Moun-
          tain. New York: Viking, 1980. grades 4-7
When Ida Early arrives at the Sutton door in Georgia
during the Depression, the children are delighted to
have her as a housekeeper. An unusual figure
(very tall, wearing bib overalls, a patched brown
sweater, and brogans), Ida immediately puts life
into the household. Ida is so cheerful and easy-
going that the children believe that "nothing could

ever get the best of Ida"--until one day at school, some of the children begin to ridicule Ida while two of the Sutton children allow the taunting to continue. Though Ida's personality changes and she acts and dresses more like other people, the children know that it isn't natural for her and long for the "old Ida." Ida leaves the family, but when she returns to her "true friends," she is her original spirited self, and the children realize the value of individuality.

193   **Burch, Robert. Queenie Peavy. New York: Viking, 1966. grades 4-7
A very independent person, Queenie Peavy, a thirteen-year-old girl, believes that when her father gets out of jail everything will be all right and she won't get into trouble anymore. However, when her father returns home, she discovers that it is really up to her to decide her future.

194   *Calhoun, Mary. Katie John. New York: Harper, 1960. grades 3-6
Individualistic ("head strong" her mother says), self-confident Katie John knows what she likes. When her family leaves California to come to Missouri to sell her Great-aunt Emily's house, ten-year-old Katie John is glad it's only temporary. But, she begins to love the old brick house and finds a way for her family to stay. Honestly, Katie John!, Depend on Katie John, and Katie John and Heathcliff are sequels.

195   *Calhoun, Mary. Ownself. New York: Harper & Row, 1975. grades 4-7
Living in Missouri in 1903 and entranced with the idea of fairies, eleven-year-old Laurabelle finds the courage to summon a fairy using the spell in a book of Welsh folklore. In an effort to regain her father's love and happiness and keep her pride, Laurabelle sees a fairy. With the fairy's help, Laurabelle gains courage to talk to her father, daydreams about being an opera singer, fills the church with hearts and flowers, and visits a band of gypsies.

196   **Calvert, Patricia. The Snowbird. New York: Scribner, 1980. grades 5+
In 1883, thirteen-year-old Willanna and her six-

year-old brother TJ are leaving Tennessee to live
with their aunt and uncle in the Dakota Territory.
After her parents' deaths in a fire, Willie feels
that she has "lots of parts and pieces and odds and
ends, but no whole." When a silver foal is born
to her aunt and uncle's mare, Willie names it Snowbird and begins to believe that it will change their
luck. However, with Snowbird's help, Willie learns
that she must find her own place without depending
on luck or others.

197   **Carlson, Dale. Baby Needs Shoes. New York:
       Atheneum, 1974. grades 5-7
Janet is a fifth-grader who lives with her older
scatterbrained sister Julie in New York. Janet is
supposed to be able to depend on Julie, but actually
it's the other way around. Janet's main concern is
getting Peter to marry Julie so they can adopt her
and not have to worry about the social worker taking
Janet away. Janet earns money to keep the family
solvent by predicting numbers in crap games and
horse racing for Fat Charlie. However, when Fat
Charlie's Chicago boss tells him to get some account
books, Janet helps Fat Charlie open the safe out of
friendship and with his promise to get her out of
the game. The gang is caught during their attempt
and given short jail sentences. Janet is placed in
Julie's custody until Peter marries Julie and can
start adoption proceedings.

198   *Carris, Joan Davenport. The Revolt of 10-X. New
       York: Harcourt Brace Jovanovich, 1980.
       grades 5-9
Attempting to deal with her father's death, thirteen-
year-old Taylor seeks the companionship of 10-X,
a computer she and her father had built. When
Taylor and her mother move to a new house, Taylor
accidentally discovers that she can control the
electricity with 10-X and tries to change her mother's
mind about moving. However, Taylor uses her
power foolishly. Upon learning that she has been
selfish in coping with her grief, Taylor begins to
accept reality, acquires a friend, finds a substitute
for her father, and uses 10-X for more constructive
purposes.

199   *Cleary, Beverly. Beezus and Ramona. New York:

Dell, 1955. grades 4-6
Nine-year-old Beezus thinks that Ramona, her four-
year-old sister, is exasperating, perfectly impossible,
and a pest. Imaginative and spirited, Ramona enter-
tains the reader with a series of hilarious escapades
in which she goes to the library with bunny ears,
locks her friend's dog in the bathroom, and bakes a
rubber doll in her sister's birthday cake. Beverly
Cleary has written a series of Ramona books, each
dealing with successive years in Ramona's life.

200   *Cleaver, Vera and Bill. Delpha Green & Company.
        Philadelphia: Lippincott, 1972. grades 7+
Thirteen-year-old Delpha helps her father found The
Church of Blessed Hope in a very small community
(Chinquapin Cove) where the weather is the most
talked-about subject. The only industry is run by
Merlin Choate, the most powerful man in town.
"The town is dead and waiting to be covered up"
when Delpha begins to tell how astrology can help
people understand themselves and others. As the
church begins to put life and sense into the town,
Mr. Choate decides to raze the church-house because it is threatening his power. However, the
Greens are offered one of two Quonset huts for
their church-house while the other one is used to
form a new business. When Mr. Choate tries to
have his wife committed to a mental institution, the
town unites to sign her petition attesting to her
sanity, keeping Mr. and Mrs. Choate together, and
effectively stalemating Mr. Choate's efforts.

201   *Cleaver, Vera and Bill. Dust of the Earth. Phil-
        adelphia: Lippincott, 1975. grades 7+
At fourteen, Fern begins to question the meaning of
her life and that of her family. Always poor, the
family unexpectedly inherits a house and land in the
early 1900s. Although the family was forever
clashing, they find they must unite and make individual sacrifices to face the challenges and overcome the hardships of life in the Black Hills. They
discover the need to know each other as well as
themselves.

202   **Cleaver, Vera and Bill. Lady Ellen Grae. Phil-
        adelphia: Lippincott, 1968. grades 4-6
According to Grover, Ellen Grae's best friend, Ellen

is not like most girls. She tells stories (lies, her
father says), fishes, climbs trees, rescues drowning
people, rows a boat, is careless about her appear-
ance, and is completely uninhibited (according to
her father). Although her parents are divorced,
they communicate freely and decide that Ellen Grae
should live with her aunt to have a good home life
and be brought up properly. Ellen Grae tries very
hard to dissuade her father and to act properly, but
she is sent to her aunt anyway. Ellen Grae is
more than her aunt anticipates, and her parents
decide that a family should be kept together, so
Ellen Grae returns home. This is the sequel to
Ellen Grae.

203   *Cleaver, Vera and Bill. Queen of Hearts. Phil-
           adelphia: Lippincott, 1978. grades 7+
       At twelve, Wilma is mildly indifferent and has
       "never been asked to make any big emotional re-
       sponses." However, when her grandmother has a
       stroke, Wilma is required to make decisions con-
       cerning her grandmother's health and companionship.
       At first, she unwillingly accepts the responsibility
       for her grandmother's care, but finally discovers
       that she really cares about Granny for her mental
       as well as her physical state.

204   *Cleaver, Vera and Bill. Where the Lilies Bloom.
           Philadelphia: Lippincott, 1969. grades 4-9
       Living in the Great Smoky Mountains, fourteen-
       year-old Mary Call, her brother, sisters, and
       father are tenant farmers on a small acreage.
       Their father's health deteriorates. Mary Call and
       the other children take care of him as well as they
       can but worry about their future if he should die.
       When they find their landlord in a shivering fit,
       they doctor him, and get him to sign a paper
       leaving their house and land to them. Their father
       dies, and it is up to Mary Call to keep the family
       together with dignity. It is then that Mary Call
       decides that they will "wildcraft"--gather plants,
       herbs, and roots for medicines--for their money
       to plant crops.

205   *Cleaver, Vera and Bill. The Whys and Wherefores
           of Littabelle Lee. New York: Atheneum, 1973.
           grades 7+

Littabelle lives with her grandparents and a maiden
aunt, a nature doctor. The summer she is sixteen,
the house burns down, all the stored food is gone,
Aunt Sorrow goes to live with the Hermit, and
Littabelle is forced to "consider her whys and wherefores." She gets a job as the deputy schoolkeeper
in order to support her grandparents and herself.
In the winter when things are getting extremely hard,
Littabelle decides to bring suit against three other
aunts and uncles for parent-neglect. She wins the
case. Determined to have a better future for herself, Littabelle finds a way to become a proper
teacher.

206   *Clements, Bruce. Anywhere Else but Here. New
          York: Farrar, Straus & Giroux, 1980. grades
          5+
       After her father's printing business goes bankrupt,
       thirteen-year-old Molly thinks that they should move
       to a new town and begin again. Her widowed father
       feels that it is too risky. When Fostra Lee Post
       and her disagreeable son visit, Molly sees that Mrs.
       Post is very interested in their family and succeeds
       in making plans for herself and her father.

207   Colman, Hila. Daughter of Discontent. New York:
          Morrow, 1971. grades 7+
       Having been brought up in an independent, matri-
       archal family, seventeen-year-old Katherine has
       never really known her father. When her father
       invites her to New York City for the summer,
       Katherine sees it as an opportunity to have the
       father-daughter relationship she has missed and a
       chance to live in a city. Although she is disappointed
       in her hopes, Katherine begins to know herself and
       others as human beings with feelings.

208   Colman, Hila. Diary of a Frantic Kid Sister. New
          York: Crown, 1973. grades 3-6
       An eleven-year-old girl feels that her older sister
       receives more attention and gets her way more
       often than she does. In coming to understand her
       sister better, she decides that she may actually
       have it easier than her sister, that her sister is
       not so bad after all, and that the two of them are
       different people and can't be compared.

209 *Conford, Ellen. Dreams of Victory. Boston:
Little, Brown, 1973. grades 4-6
Eleven-year-old Victory enjoys daydreaming. In
her fantasies, she experiences the feelings of success
that she cannot achieve in reality--President of the
United States, winner of a beauty contest, woman
astronaut, and an Oscar-winner. However, one of
her daydreams does begin to point toward real success when Victory writes an excellent composition
on imagination.

210 *Conford, Ellen. Felicia the Critic. Boston: Little,
Brown, 1973. grades 4-6
No matter what someone else says, Felicia feels
obligated to offer her critical opinion. Her mother
tells her about constructive criticism, and Felicia
thinks that maybe her future lies in being a critic.
Her first piece of constructive criticism--organizing
her mother's broom closet--is successful. Her
other efforts have varying degrees of success, as
Felicia discovers that it is difficult (nearly impossible) to determine when to give advice.

211 Conford, Ellen. Me and the Terrible Two. Boston:
Little, Brown, 1974. grades 4-7
When Dorrie's best friend moves to Australia,
eleven-year-old twin boys move in next door and
disturb her Saturday-morning sleep, tease her, and
talk like character actors. The worst seems to
have happened when she and one of the twins are
assigned to a committee for a class assignment.
Despite problems, the committee successfully pub-
lishes a special newspaper that gains them local as
well as class recognition, and Dorrie and the twins
discover the true nature of friendship.

212 **Constant, Alberta Wilson. Does Anybody Care
About Lou Emma Miller? New York: Crowell,
1979. grades 5-8
Fifteen-year-old Lou Emma, her mother, sister,
and the other women of the town (along with a few
men) meet to campaign for and elect the first woman mayor of Gloriosa. Lou Emma believes that
Mrs. Biddle's mayoral campaign should focus on
the issue of a town library; however, when her
idea is dismissed, Lou Emma sets out to begin a
library herself. This is a sequel to The Motoring

Millers and Those Miller Girls.

213   *Corcoran, Barbara. "Me and You and a Dog Named
          Blue." New York: Atheneum, 1979. grades
          5-9
       Sixteen-year-old Maggie lives with her disabled
       father. Since she is a good player on her school's
       coed baseball team, her secret wish is to go to a
       baseball training camp in Ohio. She thinks she may
       get the opportunity when she meets a woman who
       raises and shows Kerry blue terriers. Coco Rain-
       bolt offers Maggie a summer job grooming and car-
       ing for the dogs and touring with her. Maggie finds
       that her father, Coco, and her Aunt Myrt want to
       run her life, but she needs to discover herself.

214   *Corcoran, Barbara. Sam. New York: Atheneum,
          1967. grades 5-9
       Living on an island with only her parents and
       brother, fifteen-year-old Sam longs to experience
       people and places. Having been taught by her
       father, Sam is attending public school for the first
       time and wants to be accepted by others. After
       winning dog shows, fighting wolves with her bare
       hands, and refusing to "squeal" on her fellow stu-
       dents, Sam is a heroine and accepted by her class-
       mates, but not at the expense of her self-respect.

215   *Corcoran, Barbara. This Is a Recording. New
          York: Atheneum, 1971. grades 5-9
       Since her parents are leaving for Europe, fourteen-
       year-old Marianne is to stay with her grandmother
       in Montana. Marianne isn't prepared for either
       her atypical, decisive grandmother or her friendship
       and concern for two Indian boys. Playing vital
       parts in two rescues, Marianne illustrates her
       sense of justice as well as her concern and under-
       standing for others.

216   *Crane, William B. Oom-Pah. New York: Athe-
          neum, 1981. grades 5-8
       A junior in a Buena Vista, California, band, Dar-
       leen is one of two sousaphone players. Although
       the other bass player is needed for balance in the
       band and is good looking, he is constantly teasing
       Darleen about being "a little ole frail" girl "playin'
       oom-pah." She thinks he is an "impossible oaf" and

dislikes him. However, near the end of the school
year, she discovers that he has been teasing her
just to get a rise out of her and, in fact, has always
liked her. They declare a truce and find that they
can be good friends.

217 **Cresswell, Helen. Ordinary Jack. New York:
     Macmillan, 1977. grades 5+
Eleven-year-old Jack is the only ordinary member
of the talented and eccentric Bagthorpe family.
Every other Bagthorpe has multiple talents, which
range from Yoga, tennis, and swimming to electronics,
French, and math. In order to excel at something,
Jack (with his Uncle Parker's help) plans to become
a prophet and is highly successful. The sequels--
Absolute Zero, Bagthorpes Unlimited, and Bagthorpes
v. the World--continue the crazy and zany antics
of the Bagthorpe family that includes unpredictable
Grandma and cousin Daisy.

218 Crompton, Anne Eliot. A Woman's Place. Boston:
     Little, Brown, 1978. grades 7+
Tracing five generations of women at a critical time
in each woman's life, A Woman's Place tells of
subtle changes in the feminine image from the mid-
eighteenth century to the mid-twentieth century. A
Woman's Place deals with issues women face--physi-
cal survival, death, lust, loneliness, marriage or
career, love, and working motherhood.

219 **Cummings, Betty Sue. Hew Against the Grain.
     New York: Atheneum, 1977. grades 6-9
Living in Virginia during the Civil War, fourteen-
year-old Mattilda and her family are caught in the
politics, morality, and sympathies of the war. As
the war continues, Mattilda finds her family slipping
away from each other through death and grief. Her
grandfather calls it "dwindling--a shrinking of the
spirit and a giving up." Mattilda vows to "stop the
family from falling back" until she is more person-
ally affected by the war--she is raped--and she
considers suicide. With her grandfather's support
and his advice to "hew against the grain--take her
worries one at a time and live them," Mattilda
finds the strength to continue living the tough reality.

220 **Cunningham, Julia. Flight of the Sparrow. New
     York: Pantheon, 1980. grades 5-9

Fourteen-year-old Mago finds nine-year-old Little
Cigarette in her second orphanage, invites her to
join him in the streets of Paris, and gives her the
courage to survive. To get some money to help a
friend, Cigarette steals a valuable painting from an
artist friend, and Mago sells it. Cigarette finds that
she must leave Paris to make things right--to save
Mago from being blackmailed and to ask forgiveness
from the artist. When Cigarette finds her artist
friend, it is too late--the police have a sketch of
her, and Mago has been identified. However, Cigarette has a chance for a new life as she decides to
live with a woman who has befriended her.

221   *Curry, Jane Louise. Parsley, Sage, Rosemary &
          Time. New York: Atheneum, 1975. grades
          3-7
      Sent to live with her aunt for a short time, ten-
      year-old Rosemary discovers four stones in her
      aunt's backyard that say Parsley, Sage, Rosemary,
      and Time. Upon further investigation, she finds
      that when she touches the herb surrounding the
      Time stone, Time stops for everyone but her.
      Then, one day, she eats a sprig of the herb and
      finds herself back in the eighteenth century just
      before a witchcraft trial.

222   *Danziger, Paula. Can You Sue Your Parents for
          Malpractice? New York: Delacorte, 1979.
          grades 5-9
      Between her parents, two sisters, and school,
      fourteen-year-old Lauren feels that she has no
      rights. When she registers for a class entitled
      "Law for Children and Young People," Lauren
      anticipates suing her parents for malpractice. She
      learns instead that her problems have other solutions
      and that she can survive if she does what is best
      for her in spite of what others think.

223   *Danziger, Paula. The Cat Ate My Gymsuit. New
          York: Delacorte, 1974. grades 5-9
      Thirteen-year-old Marcy has several problems--
      school, her father, her weight problem, and acne.
      Things begin to change for the better when Ms.
      Finney is hired as an English teacher. With Ms.
      Finney's concern and help, Marcy learns to feel
      more secure and independent. When Ms. Finney is

fired, Marcy helps to organize a protest and is
suspended for it. However, although Ms. Finney
resigns after being reinstated, Marcy realizes the
meaning of empathy.

224   *Darke, Marjorie. A Question of Courage. New
       York: Crowell, 1975. grades 6-12
Eighteen-year-old Emily finds herself getting very
involved in the women's-suffrage movement in Great
Britain in the early 1900s. When the movement
turns violent, Emily participates but questions the
tactics and seeks to accomplish the same end through
nonviolence.

225   *Douglass, Barbara. Skateboard Scramble. Phila-
       delphia: Westminster, 1979. grades 5-7
Having just moved, Jody finds that her father insists on her entering the Skateboard Scramble his
company is cosponsoring. Jody doesn't know how
to tell her father that she is afraid to perform for
a group, since he expects her to win. However,
she meets Carmen, who is also scared but desper-
ately wants the first prize. Jody learns that there
is more than one way to be a champion when she
overcomes her fear and places second to Carmen.

226   **Duncombe, Frances. Summer of the Burning. New
       York: Putnam, 1976. grades 5-9
Living in Bedford, New York, in 1779, thirteen-
year-old Hannah and her family wonder when their
father will be exchanged for some British prisoners.
Before he returns, their house is burned by the
Hessians, their mother dies just after childbirth,
and an older brother refuses to help with the family
chores. It is up to Hannah to keep the family together, make plans to rebuild the house, and do
her patriotic duty to see that cattle are safely de-
livered to the American troops.

227   *Embry, Margaret. Kid Sister. New York:
       Scholastic, 1967. grades 3-6
Ten-year-old Zib volunteers to care for a baby
hooded rat. Despite her older sister's disapproval,
Zib receives help and support from her parents.
Although Rosemary (the rat) manages to disturb
the household and school at times, events proceed
normally until Great-aunt Delia is asked to stay

with Zib's family. Zib is faced with having to get
rid of Rosemary until she accidentally discovers
that her great-aunt enjoys her unusual pet.

228   **Engebrecht, P. A.   Under the Haystack.   Nashville,
         Tenn.: Nelson, 1973.   grades 6+
      Thirteen-year-old Sandy discovers that her parents
      have deserted her and her sisters. At first, Sandy
      invents a story of her mother visiting a sick aunt.
      However, when the neighbors become suspicious
      and the youngest girl discovers the truth, they
      depend more on each other for cooperation in main-
      taining the small farm. Rather than run from the
      authorities, Sandy decides that they will show how
      well they have taken care of themselves. It is as
      they prepare for the sheriff that their mother re-
      turns.

229   *Feil, Hila.   The Windmill Summer.   New York:
         Harper & Row, 1972.   grades 3-7
      Tired of her relatives' constant complaints and
      nagging, eleven-year-old Arabella tells her parents
      that she is going to live in her great-grandfather's
      shiplike windmill in their backyard for the rest of
      the summer. Taking a few provisions with her,
      Arabella cooks and takes care of herself without
      adult intervention. At the windmill, she finds her-
      self taking responsibility for several wild animals,
      but she discovers that she cannot hope to protect
      them from all their natural enemies. As she
      prepares to return home at the end of the summer,
      Arabella better understands herself and others and
      the need for patience, love, and communication.

230   *Fitzhugh. Louise.   The Long Secret.   New York:
         Harper & Row, 1965.   grades 5+
      Harriet (a sixth-grader) wants to become a writer,
      so she constantly carries a notebook with her to
      record her observations of and reactions to people
      on whom she spies. When everyone in town begins
      to receive mysterious messages, Harriet decides
      to solve the mystery. However, Harriet finds the
      problem difficult to resolve and is amazed when
      she is forced to conclude the obvious but seemingly
      unreasonable truth--her shy girlfriend is the cul-
      prit. This is a sequel to Harriet the Spy.

231   *Flory, Jane. <u>The Golden Venture.</u> Boston: Hough-
          ton Mifflin, 1967. grades 4-6
       Minnie has lived with her father and her Aunt Addie
       all her eleven years since her mother died in child-
       birth. When her father decides to head for the
       goldfields in 1850, Minnie stows away in the wagon
       and is on her way to San Francisco. In San Fran-
       cisco, Minnie meets Mrs. Stanhope and Daisy Pal-
       mer, two very unconventional women, and they
       successfully establish a business on a docked ship.

232   *Flory, Jane. <u>The Liberation of Clementine Tipton.</u>
          Boston: Houghton Mifflin, 1974. grades 3-7
       It's the year of the centennial, 1876, and Philadel-
       phia is bustling with activity. Ten-year-old Clemen-
       tine is being schooled in the proper dress and be-
       havior for a young lady, but she has other ideas.
       She and a cousin rent a pony and cart for a lively
       ride, and they decide to earn money by cleaning
       the horses' stalls in their good clothes.

233   Freeman, Barbara C. <u>A Pocket of Silence.</u> New
          York: Dutton, 1977. grades 4-7
       On her sixteenth birthday, Caroline feels that for
       some reason she must return to her childhood
       home. Through a time warp, she meets Zilia and
       is able to fill some of the "pockets of silence"
       concerning the strange disappearance of a young
       girl many years before, which is intertwined with
       Caroline's own ancestral history.

234   **Garden, Nancy. <u>Fours Crossing.</u> New York:
          Farrar, Straus & Giroux, 1981. grades 6+
       Still attempting to cope with her mother's death,
       thirteen-year-old Melissa comes to live with her
       grandmother in Fours Crossing, New Hampshire,
       while her father concludes his business. She
       arrives in time to participate in the Spring Festival.
       However, the heavy blizzards, a missing antique
       silver plate, a mysterious golden dog, a strange
       hermit, and missing town archives combine to pre-
       sent Melissa and her friend Jed with questions and
       suspicions. In solving the mystery, Melissa and
       Jed find that they are also able to face their own
       problems.

235   **Gartner, Chloe. <u>Anne Bonny.</u> New York: Morrow,

1977. grades 7+
Moving from Ireland to London to the Carolinas in
the New World, Anne and her family enjoy a pros-
perous life in the 1700s. Anne has enjoyed all the
advantages her successful lawyer-businessman father
could provide. When her father arranges her marriage to another wealthy businessman's son, Anne
decides that she will take charge of her own life.
She marries another man and then runs away with
him to become a pirate.

236 **Gartner, Chloe. The Woman from the Glen. New
York: Morrow, 1973. grades 7+
Jennie and Pollux, twenty-four-year-old twins in
the Scottish Highlands, believe that their destinies
are intertwined with that of the exiled Stuart prince,
Prince Charles, since they were born at the same
hour. Hoping to be saved from domesticity, Jennie
is overjoyed when she hears that Prince Charles has
left France to attempt to regain his family's throne
in 1745 and goes with her brother to join the Prince's
army.

237 *Gathorne-Hardy, Jonathan. Operation Peeg. Philadelphia: Lippincott, 1972. grades 4-9
At a dreary boarding school on the island of Peeg
off the coast of Scotland, Jane contemplates running
away to her home in London after she gets into
trouble. She gets her wish, but not quite in the
expected way, when an explosion sets the island
adrift with only Jane, her best friend, and her
housekeeper on it. Their advantage involves them
in state secrets and a master plan that could destroy an entire continent in the years before World
II.

238 *George, Jean Craighead. The Cry of the Crow.
New York: Harper & Row, 1980. grades 5+
When Mandy finds a young crow in the woods near
her home, she keeps it a secret, tames it, feeds
it, and communicates with it. However, Mandy
worries about her father shooting it and about the
hunter who killed the crow's parents. Mandy is
also torn between allowing her crow to return to
the wild and keeping it as a pet. When her crow
attacks her brother, Mandy realizes that she has
made a mistake in keeping her pet, and she must
destroy it before it hurts someone else.

239   George, Jean Craighead. <u>Hook a Fish, Catch a Mountain.</u> New York: Dutton, 1975. grades 4-7

Thirteen-year-old Spinner would prefer being back in New York City practicing her ballet, but it is a matter of family pride that she at least try to catch the largest fish and get the trophy back from her grandfather. After Spinner does catch a large cutthroat, which has become extinct in that area, she actively participates in a backpacking ecological expedition to the mountains to determine what has happened to the cutthroats.

240   *George, Jean Craighead. <u>The Summer of the Falcon.</u> New York: Crowell, 1962. grades 4+

As a member of a family who always have animals around, thirteen-year-old June wants her own pet. She is given a young, spirited sparrowhawk by her father. June works hard for a while at training him, but then becomes involved in other activities and lets the training slide. Eventually, with even more intensive training, June is able to teach her sparrowhawk to hunt and impresses even her father, who is skeptical of her ability to finish a project.

241   **Gerson, Corinne. <u>Passing Through.</u> New York: Dial, 1978. grades 9+

When Liz's brother commits suicide, Liz, who is fifteen, thinks that she will rely on herself. It seems that she can't depend on her parents for understanding since they have entirely different values, and she feels the gap between herself and her parents widening. At school, she meets Sam, who has cerebral palsy, and discovers a friend with whom she can share her feelings about herself, her parents, and her brother. Sam finds that Liz can also help him with some of his problems. Liz receives help from others, but she finds that it is up to her to put it all together to find her own solution to her problems.

242   *Glaser, Dianne. <u>The Diary of Trilby Frost.</u> New York: Holiday House, 1976. grades 6+

Living in Tennessee in 1899, Trilby receives a diary from her father for her thirteenth birthday. Calling her his "special child," her father states that the diary is to "set down her mads and her happies." Indeed, Trilby is faced with many "mads"--her father's and brother's deaths, her unmarried sister's pregnancy, and the knowledge of her own illegitimacy. However, Trilby also encounters some "happies"-- her friendship with Saul, her mischievous episodes at Miss Stuart's School of Genteel Breeding, and her closer relationships with her mother and sister. As she matures, Trilby continues to fight for her life-- to be creative and a dreamer.

243   *Green, Phyllis. Grandmother Orphan. Nashville, Tenn.: Nelson, 1977. grades 4+
Expelled from school for a week because of stealing, sixth-grader Christy is sent to visit her "bad" grandmother for punishment. At first, Christy thinks that her truck-driving, tough and feisty grandmother is the meanest person in the world. However, she discovers that her grandmother's exterior is only a cover for her loneliness as a child, and Christy finds that being adopted is not the worst fate in the world.

244   *Green, Phyllis. Mildred Murphy, How Does Your Garden Grow? Reading, Mass.: Addison-Wesley, 1977. grades 3-7
Ten-year-old Mildred has just moved from New Jersey to California with her parents. Mildred is lonely, but in exploring her surroundings (both people and places), she discovers a mystery when she develops a close relationship with an older woman whom she helps. Mildred shows others that "sometimes you only get one chance in life to help another person."

245   **Green, Phyllis. Wild Violets. Nashville, Tenn.: Nelson, 1977. grades 4+
Cornelia is the most important person in the fourth grade. Everyone likes her. Ruthie is probably the least important person in the fourth grade. No one likes her because she is very poor. Wanting to be Cornelia's friend, Ruthie has the opportunity when Cornelia's father becomes ill and the family must sell everything to pay his hospital bills. Although no one at school will play with either girl, Ruthie remains friends with Cornelia even when her mother forbids it.

246   **Greene, Constance C. Dotty's Suitcase. New York: Viking, 1980. grades 5-9
Living with her father and two older sisters during

the Depression, twelve-year-old Dotty dreams of
getting a suitcase and traveling. When she and Jud,
an eight-year-old friend, find a suitcase filled with
money, they set out to visit her best friend in another
town. While escaping from a person who wants to
take their money, they become lost in a snowstorm
and learn the meaning of friendship.

247 **Greene, Constance C. Isabelle the Itch. New York:
Viking, 1973. grades 3-7
Because Isabelle is very energetic, her mother calls
her an itch. Ten-year-old Isabelle's favorite daily
activity is to fight with Herbie, her best friend. She
wants to take over her brother's paper route, hopes
to win the fifty-yard dash, and anticipates becoming
a tap dancer or a truck driver when she grows up.
Isabelle gets her opportunity to deliver the paper and
meets Mrs. Stern, who helps Isabelle channel some
of her energy for a constructive purpose.

248 *Greenwald, Sheila. All the Way to Wits' End.
Boston: Little, Brown, 1979. grades 3-7
When her family moves, eleven-year-old Drucilla
knows she will not like the new place. She feels
strange and different with her funny old hand-me-
down clothes, furniture, and teeth ("the Bundage
mouth"). Drucilla decides to do something about
changing her image so she organizes a tag sale to
sell her things. The sale goes so well that she
convinces her parents to sell their antiques to buy
new things, but then Drucilla sees the changes as
being too drastic. She misses being different, so
she initiates another plan to save the family heritage.

249 Greenwald, Sheila. The Atrocious Two. Boston:
Houghton Mifflin, 1978. grades 4-6
Cecilia (ten years old) and Ashley (eleven) have
gained a reputation for being spoiled brats. When
their parents try to get rid of them for the month
between the end of school and the beginning of
summer camp, only Aunt Tessie and Uncle Bear
will take them. After Bear's original Indian jewelry
is stolen, Cecilia makes it her goal to find the
thief, and the "atrocious two" become more human.

250 *Greenwald, Sheila. The Mariah Delany Lending
Library Disaster. Boston: Houghton Mifflin,

1977. grades 4-6
Twelve-year-old Mariah Delany can't seem to resist
venturing into money-making enterprises. This time
she thinks she has the best idea yet. With her
parents' extensive collection of books, she creates
her own lending library and charges 2¢ a day for
overdue books. Things are fine until it is time for
the books to be returned and no one returns any!
It is up to Mariah to salvage her scheme.

251   *Groman, Gal. Gertie McMichaels Finds Blood and
            Gore and Much Much More. New York:
            McGraw-Hill, 1971. grades 4-6
        Teenaged Gertie has three suspects for the burning
        of O'Reilly's stable, where her horse was kept. Since
        the police and insurance investigators don't appear
        to be trying to solve the mystery, Gertie believes
        that she can discover the arsonist. She thinks that
        the man who wanted to buy O'Reilly's land, or
        O'Reilly's greedy stepson, or Rotten Ronnie may have
        set fire to the stable. Using detective techniques,
        Gertie sorts out the facts. Gertie McMichaels and
        the Odd Body Mystery is the sequel.

252   *Hall, Elizabeth. Stand Up, Lucy. Boston: Hough-
            ton Mifflin, 1971. grades 3-7
        Despite her father's protests, fourteen-year-old Lucy
        becomes involved in the suffrage movement at the
        turn of the century after she attends a speech given
        by her aunt.

253   Hall, Lynn. The Mystery of Pony Hollow. Cham-
            paign, Ill.: Garrard, 1978. grades 3-4
        While riding her pony in south-central Iowa, Sarah
        discovers a small stone house that contains the
        skeleton of a horse. Determined to discover how
        the horse died, Sarah searches out a relative of the
        previous farm-owner and the groom who holds the
        key to the mystery's solution.

254   *Harris, Christie. The Trouble with Princesses.
            New York: Atheneum, 1980. grades 3-7
        This collection of stories depicts the experiences
        of New World princesses. Some princesses had no
        intention of sitting in their castles waiting to be
        married. Instead, they went out and found their
        own princes. Or, other times, the princess helped

the prince to accomplish his impossible tasks. Some
princesses did not want to marry the person they
were told to marry, so they took matters into their
own hands.

255 **Hayes, Kent, and Lazzarine, Alex. <u>Broken Promise.</u>
New York: Putnam, 1978. grades 9+
Five children are abandoned by their parents fifteen
hundred miles from home. The oldest, Patty, is
eleven and has been the children's full-time babysitter and surrogate mother since she was four.
Charlie, the youngest, is eighteen months old. After
surviving by themselves for sixteen days, the police
catch them, and the entire bureaucratic system
of juvenile court, detention centers, foster homes,
penal system, state hospital, and social welfare
agencies is set in motion. The welfare of the
children is overlooked, except by one man who finds
a way to keep a promise.

256 *Hazen, Barbara Shook. <u>Amelia's Flying Machine.</u>
Garden City, N. Y.: Doubleday, 1977. grades
3-5
After hearing that the Wright brothers have just
built and flown a flying machine in 1905, Amelia
decides to build her own and show Jimmy Watson
that she can do anything he can.

257 *Hildick, E. W. <u>The Active-Enzyme Lemon-Freshened
Junior High School Witch.</u> Garden City, N. Y.:
Doubleday, 1973. grades 4-7
While recuperating from the measles, Alison discovers
a book on the secret arts of witchcraft and plans to
become a witch. Using the book as a guide, Alison
improvises and creates a witch name, a gesture of
defiance, and the sundry equipment necessary to become a witch.

258 *Hildick, E. W. <u>The Top-Flight Fully Automated
Junior High School Girl Detective.</u> Garden City,
N. Y.: Doubleday, 1977. grades 4-7
When Emmeline's father loses his Newcharge card
and is in danger of losing his job because of it,
Alison decides to help Emmeline recover it and find
the Perpetrator. Her detective techniques get them
into some unusual situations, but through deductive
reasoning, Alison and her friends are able to solve

the case. This is the sequel to <u>The Active-Enzyme Lemon-Freshened Junior High School Witch</u>.

259 **Hilgartner, Beth. <u>A Necklace of Fallen Stars.</u>
Boston: Little, Brown, 1979. grades 7+
When independent Kaela is summoned by her father
the King and told that she will marry Duke Gavrin,
Kaela vows that she will not marry him and runs
away to a distant kingdom. Kaela meets Kippen, a
young minstrel whom she sets free by using her gift
for storytelling. Enraged by her independence and
flouting of his authority, the King orders a sorcerer
to return Kaela dead or alive. Kaela and Kippen
elude the sorcerer until the message of Kaela's
father's pardon and death arrives.

260 **Hoover, H.M. <u>This Time of Darkness.</u> New York:
Viking, 1980. grades 7+
Eleven-year-old Amy has lived all of her life in the
dirty, decaying underground city. Having heard
stories about "outside," Amy has to find a way out.
When she meets Axel, who says he has lived outside, she knows that her daydream must become her
ambition. Determined to escape, Amy and Axel
risk their lives many times to find Axel's parents
and live a better life.

261 **Irwin, Hadley. <u>The Lilith Summer.</u> Old Westbury,
N.Y.: Feminist Press, 1979. grades 4-7
In order to earn money for a ten-speed bicycle,
twelve-year-old Ellen reluctantly agrees to be a
companion to seventy-seven-year-old Lilith Adams.
When each discovers that the other is being paid to
be a companion or a babysitter, they declare a truce
and discover that the generation gap can be bridged
with friendship, love, and understanding.

262 **Jacob, Helen Pierce. <u>The Secret of the Strawbridge
Place.</u> New York: Atheneum, 1976. grades
3-7
In the early 1930s, Kate is going to have a summer
vacation filled with swimming and other activities--
until she breaks her arm. Together with Oscar,
who has broken his ankle, they decide to organize
Cripples Incorporated and investigate the secret of
the Strawbridge place--a story that the Strawbridge
family was a link in the Underground Railroad. The

Diary of the Strawbridge Place is the sequel.

263   *Klein, Norma. It's Not What You Expect. New
              York: Pantheon, 1973. grades 5-9
        Oliver and Carla, fourteen-year-old twins, decide
        to open and operate a French restaurant during the
        summer months in a neighbor's house. While suc-
        cessfully establishing the restaurant, they also at-
        tempt to cope with their parents' separation, their
        brother's girlfriend's abortion, and their own sexuali-
        ty. They learn that the world is frequently dis-
        illusioning and "life is not what you expect ... what-
        ever that is."

264   Klein, Norma. Tomboy. New York: Four Winds,
              1978. grades 3-7
        Toe, short for Antonia, is a ten-year-old whose
        mother works, whose father is unemployed and works
        as a househusband, whose best friend is a boy, and
        who wants to be a radio announcer or a dog trainer.
        Toe finds that being called a tomboy may not really
        mean anything because it "does not really include
        or exclude any specific behaviors."

265   **Knudson, R.R. You Are the Rain. New York:
              Delacorte, 1974. grades 7+
        The second all-girl tour allowed to canoe a hundred
        miles on the Flamingo River in the Florida Ever-
        glades includes Crash and Rollie, who are physically
        prepared for the trip, and June, who is ridiculed
        for quoting poetry. Crash and June are separated
        from the group during a hurricane. They learn
        respect for each other when Crash is bitten by a
        coral snake and her life depends on June, who
        successfully performs the necessary tasks.

266   **Knudson, R.R. Zanballer. New York: Delacorte,
              1972. grades 7+
        When the school's gymnasium is rebuilt just before
        basketball season, Zan (Suzanne) protests to the
        principal but without success. Since the gym is
        unavailable, the eighth-grade girls' gym class is
        scheduled in the home-ec room for dance. Zan
        decides to skip class and talks the boys' football
        coach into letting her use the lacrosse field for
        practice. When Zan finds enough friends for a
        football team, they practice and are allowed to play

a game against the boys' team. Zanbanger, Zan-
boomer, and Rinehart Lifts are sequels.

267   *Konigsburg, E. L.   About the B'nai Bagels.   New
            York: Atheneum, 1969.   grades 3-7
Mark's mother, Bess, begins having problems with
Spencer, her older son, when he goes to college
and begins arguing with her about everything. Bess
feels she needs an outlet for her energy, so she
becomes the manager of a boys' Little League team
sponsored by the B'nai B'rith Sisterhood. The problems she meets in dealing with mothers, strategy,
her coach son, baseball talent or lack of it, and
concern for the team are amusing as well as serious.

268   **Konigsburg, E. L.   From the Mixed-Up Files of
            Mrs. Basil E. Frankweiler.   New York:
            Atheneum, 1967.   grades 3-7
The oldest of four children and the only girl, eleven-
year-old Claudia feels unfairly treated by her parents
and bored with the monotony of everything.   For
weeks, she saves her allowance and makes plans to
run away from her home in Greenwich to the Metropolitan
Museum of Art in New York City.   Claudia decides
to take her nine-year-old brother, Jamie, along with
her because he has money.   For a week, they evade
the guards at the museum.   However, Claudia discovers that she really wants an adventure that will
help her to feel differently inside--she is determined
to discover the unknown sculptor of a statue.   When
Claudia and Jamie succeed in unraveling the secret,
they return home having gained maturity.

269   *Konigsburg, E. L.   Jennifer, Hecate, Macbeth,
            William McKinley, and Me, Elizabeth.   New
            York: Atheneum, 1968.   grades 3-8
When she and her family move to the suburbs of
New York City, Elizabeth (a fifth-grader) doesn't
have any friends until she meets Jennifer, who
claims to be a witch.   While her mother is concerned about Elizabeth's apparent lack of friends
and her "normality," the girls secretly meet every
Saturday so Elizabeth can study to become an apprentice witch.   As the girls approach the final test
for becoming a "proper witch," Elizabeth and Jennifer have an argument.   The disagreement makes
them aware of their loneliness, and they find that

they "enjoy being what they really are ... just
good friends. "

270   *Ladd, Elizabeth. Marty Runs Away to Sea. New
      York: Morrow, 1968. grades 3-7
      Ten-year-old Marty lives with her father on an
      island off the coast of Maine, where they dig clams
      and lobsters to sell. When Marty's father is in-
      jured in a boating accident, Marty is sent to live
      with her Aunt Tilly, who vows to curtail Marty's
      freedom and teach her to act like a lady. Marty
      decides to leave her aunt and runs away on a cruise
      ship. When her aunt finds her, she continues plan-
      ning Marty's future, but a friend intervenes to re-
      unite Marty and her father.

271   *Ladd, Elizabeth. Meg of Heron's Neck. New York:
      Morrow, 1961. grades 3-7
      Ten-year-old Meg has stayed with her older half-
      brother, Allen, since their parents died two years
      ago. Living aboard an old skiff, they are free to
      come and go as they please. One day, her uncle
      arrives at the dock to take Meg to live with his
      family. Allen knows that legally her uncle can
      take Meg, and he leaves. Determined to stay with
      Allen, Meg vows to cause so much trouble that her
      uncle will take her back. However, she begins to
      accept her new home and realizes that her half-
      brother really cannot take care of her.

272   *Langton, Jane. The Boyhood of Grace Jones. New
      York: Harper & Row, 1972. grades 5+
      Living just after the Depression, twelve-year-old
      Grace Jones is known for her "vital spark" and
      "careless rapture"--or what others call being a
      tomboy. She wears her father's Navy middy blouse
      over her dress, climbs trees, and "is" Trueblue
      Tom, the first mate of the ship The Flying Cloud.
      Grace is determined to be herself and not be domi-
      nated by either heredity or environment. This is
      a sequel to The Majesty of Grace.

273   *Langton, Jane. The Diamond in the Window. New
      York: Harper & Row, 1962. grades 5+
      Living with their aunt and uncle, Eleanor and Ed-
      ward notice a keyhole-shaped window in one of the
      towers of the house. After some investigation, they

discover the way into the tower and find a small
bedroom, arranged for children. Their aunt then
tells them the story of their namesakes, Uncle Ned
and Aunt Nora, who disappeared as children. Eleanor and Edward vow to solve the mystery of their
disappearance and discover a poem scratched on the
keyhole window that tells of diamonds, rubies, and
other treasures that could save their house from
being sold.

274   Lawrence, Mildred. Peachtree Island. New York:
          Harcourt, Brace & World, 1948. grades 3-6
       Nine-year-old Cissie can't remember her mother
       and father, but she can remember all the aunts she
       has lived with. Now, she is sent to visit her Uncle
       Eben on Peachtree Island. When Cissie overhears
       her uncle say that if she were a boy he'd keep her
       forever, Cissie determines to do the work of a
       boy--gassing, trimming, raking, planting, and
       picking the peach trees. However, with all her
       anxiety and hard work, Cissie finds that her uncle
       was teasing about wanting a boy, and she finally
       has a permanent home.

275   **Lawrence, Mildred. Touchmark. New York: Har-
          court Brace Jovanovich, 1975. grades 4-7
       Recently orphaned, fourteen-year-old Nabby wishes
       to become apprenticed to a pewterer in Boston in
       1773. Hoping to find her own apprenticeship, Nabby
       inquires about her prospects. Nabby agrees to be
       bound to the pewterer as a servant, but always
       with the hope and determination to become appren-
       ticed to him. Just before the Revolution, Nabby
       finds herself an observer and messenger for the
       patriot cause and eventually achieves her goal of
       becoming a pewterer's apprentice.

276   Lawrence, Mildred. The Treasure and the Song.
          New York: Harcourt Brace & World, 1966.
          grades 7+
       When seventeen-year-old Binnie is told that her
       parents are getting a divorce, she decides to pack
       up her things and live in Florida with an aunt she
       hasn't seen in seven years. Using her guitar to
       express her feelings, Binnie prefers to be isolated,
       but a shy girl looks to her for guidance and con-
       fidence, and two boys involve her in a search for
       buried treasure.

277   *Lawrence, Mildred. Walk a Rocky Road. New
York: Harcourt Brace Jovanovich, 1971.
grades 7+
A high school senior, Silvy thoughtlessly says that
she plans to go to college to become a teacher.
Her pride will not let her retract her statement.
However, her problem is in getting the money without expecting any help from her parents. Living in
the Appalachian mountains, Silvy and Kel discover
that they share a common goal--wanting to break
out of a dying way of life. They work together on a
rare-earth mineral project, for which they receive
scholarships and opportunities for better lives.

278   *Lee, Beverly Haskell. The Secret of Van Rink's
Cellar. Minneapolis: Lerner, 1979. grades
4-9
Living in colonial New York in 1780, eleven-year-
old Sarah and her nine-year-old brother, Stephen,
are intrigued by stories about a ghost haunting the
house in which they live. They investigate the
cellar for evidence of the ghost and discover dried
muddy footprints. When their mother becomes ill,
she reveals to Sarah that she has been a spy for
General Washington and solicits her cooperation in
sending a final message. After their mother leaves
New York to recuperate, Sarah and Stephen unravel
the identity of their "ghost" and continue to spy.
When their situation becomes too precarious, they
are reunited with their mother.

279   *Levitin, Sonia. The No-Return Trail. New York:
Harcourt Brace Jovanovich, 1978. grades 7+
Seventeen-year-old Nancy is determined to accompany her husband, Ben, from Missouri to California
in 1841. With her baby, Nancy endures illness,
lack of food and water, boredom, fatigue, loneliness, and doubt to become the first woman to make
the journey overland. This is the fictionalized
account of the 1841 Bidwell-Bartleson expedition,
which included Nancy Kelsey.

280   *Levitin, Sonia. Rita the Weekend Rat. New York:
Atheneum, 1971. grades 3-5
Rita (a real rat) becomes a weekend rat when seven-
year-old Cynthia takes her home to care for her on
the weekends. However, Cynthia doesn't always

finish what she starts. When Cynthia gets an opportunity to keep Rita, she has to show she is responsible. At the same time, Cynthia is also involved in
being president of the Boys Club she started, organizing a paper drive, and showing her older
brother how to tie knots. Cynthia finds that she
can be responsible, finish projects, have both boys
and girls as friends, and be anything she wants to be.

281 Levy, Elizabeth. The Tryouts. New York: Four
Winds, 1979. grades 4-7
When the principal of Grover Cleveland Grammar
School decides to allow girls to try out for the
junior high basketball team, students, parents, and
coach must deal with their feelings about a possible
coed team. Donna and Janet make the team, but
Diggy, who has played for three years, is cut. This
poses a dilemma for everyone, which they solve by
negotiating a student-assistant coach position for
Diggy.

282 *Lewis, C.S. The Lion, the Witch and the Wardrobe.
New York: Macmillan, 1950. grades 4-6
During World War II, Peter, Susan, Edmund, and
Lucy are sent from London to live with an old professor. It is Lucy, the youngest, who discovers
that the old wardrobe in an otherwise empty room
is the entrance to Narnia, a world where the evil
White Witch has made it winter just before Christmas forever. Edmund also finds his way into
Narnia, where he meets the White Witch, who per-
suades him to leave Narnia but to return with his
brother and sisters. She promises that he will
become the Prince. The children go to Narnia to
help Aslan, the lion king, triumph over the White
Witch and become the Kings and Queens of Narnia
until they return to the real world. Six sequels
complete the Chronicles of Narnia.

283 *Love, Sandra. But What About Me? New York:
Harcourt Brace Jovanovich, 1976. grades 3-7
Just before Lucy's eleventh birthday, her mother
goes back to work. Lucy circles that date on her
calendar in black because she wants her mother to
stay home. When things change more than Lucy
could have imagined, she dislikes all the changes.
However, she discovers that growing up isn't easy,

but "letting go of old things isn't so hard when she knows there are new things coming her way."

284 *Lutters, Valerie A. The Haunting of Julie Unger. New York: Atheneum, 1977. grades 7+
Twelve-year-old Julie and her father enjoyed a close and special relationship, especially when they shared their photography sessions. When her father suddenly dies and the family moves, Julie is denied her only friends. Always having been a loner, Julie at first denies her photography but later secretly goes to the place where she and her father had gone to take pictures. Here, she imagines her father's presence. Eventually, Julie realizes real friendship through her photography and is able to face life without her father.

285 *McCord, Jean. Turkeylegs Thompson. New York: Atheneum, 1979. grades 4-8
After twelve-year-old Betty Ann tries to join the boys' basketball team, one of the boys begins calling her Turkeylegs. Even Betty Ann thinks of herself as Turkey, and her motto is "I'm tough and I'm going to stay that way!" However, since her parents have been divorced, her mother has to work "to keep them together." Feeling angry and lonely, Turkey has to care for her younger brother and sister, which leaves her little time of her own. In addition to her anger against life and power, Turkey must deal with her theft of a bicycle, the death of her sister, and the return of her father. After a period of uncertainty, Turkey decides that "there were things waiting in the world for her," and she optimistically determines to "fill in the empty spaces of her life."

286 **Miles, Betty. The Real Me. New York: Knopf, 1974. grades 3+
When eleven-year-old Barbara has to select a PE class listed for girls (slimnastics) instead of taking tennis (for boys), she attempts to get support for a change in the PE program by circulating a petition. At the same time, she learns that girls are not allowed to deliver the newspaper. Determined to remove these obstacles, she sets a course to become a pioneer for girls' rights, with some success.

287   *Milton, Hilary. <u>The Brats and Mr. Jack</u>. New
           York: Beaufort, 1980. grades 6+
       Thirteen-year-old Meg and twelve-year-old Yancy,
       sister and brother, run away from the Carson County
       Home, determined to live on their own. Befriended
       by an unusual "bum," Mr. Jack, who tells them of
       a place to live, the children get odd jobs and use
       their imaginations to earn money and food without
       begging or getting into trouble. Mr. Jack and the
       children become friends and discover that they can
       help each other while still retaining their indepen-
       dence.

288   **Minard, Rosemary, ed. <u>Womenfolk and Fairy Tales</u>.
           Boston: Houghton Mifflin, 1975. grades 2-5
       The feminine heroines in these tall tales are active,
       intelligent, capable, and courageous human beings.

289   **Montgomery, L. M. <u>Anne of Green Gables</u>. New
           York: Farrar, Straus & Giroux, 1908. grades
           5-8
       At the turn of the century, eleven-year-old Anne is
       mistakenly sent from an orphan asylum to Matthew
       and Marilla on Prince Edward Island in Newfound-
       land. They had wanted a boy to help them on their
       farm, since they were getting older, but Anne's
       sparkle and enthusiasm for life and beauty change
       their minds, and she is allowed to stay. Anne's
       unpredictable speech and behavior, imagination, and
       creativity cause everyone problems. There are
       several sequels that follow Anne into adulthood.

290   *Morgenroth, Barbara. <u>Impossible Charlie</u>. New
           York: Atheneum, 1979. grades 4-6
       Jackie's parents aren't interested in her wanting to
       ride and jump horses. Her father will not consent
       to buying a horse, since they are so expensive.
       But when Jackie is offered a horse for free, he
       does agree. Jackie thinks he is the perfect horse,
       and she will be able to really ride and jump. How-
       ever, she finds that Charlie has a mind of his own,
       and there is "more to riding than just jumping on
       and galloping across fields." By the end of the
       summer, Jackie is determined to accept the chal-
       lenge of handling Impossible Charlie and discovers
       that he is "sort of possible after all."

291   *Morgenroth, Barbara. <u>Last Junior Year</u>. New
          York: Atheneum, 1978. grades 5-9
       Seventeen-year-old Kim wants to become a member
       of the United States equestrian team. Her mother
       and father show little interest in her choice of
       careers and, in fact, seek to discourage her selec-
       tion. Her choice is complicated by the fact that
       her family is not wealthy and cannot afford the ex-
       penses involved. However, Kim is so determined to
       achieve her goal that she finds her own ways to
       learn to ride and show her horse.

292   **Murphy, Shirley Rousseau. <u>Soonie and the Dragon</u>.
          New York: Atheneum, 1979. grades 4-6
       In the first of three stories comprising this book,
       Soonie rescues three princesses from a dragon when
       the women's true loves are so cowardly they do not
       attempt the rescue. In the second story, Soonie is
       trapped by a fairy king who unsuccessfully tries to
       make her his wife with magic potions. In her
       search for a young man to love in the third story,
       Soonie knows what she thinks about things so she
       will not settle for a handsome man who can sing
       and dance but who lacks kindness, consideration,
       and helpfulness.

293   *North, Joan. <u>The Light Maze.</u> New York: Farrar,
          Straus & Giroux, 1971. grades 7+
       Harriet's father, Tom Nancarrow, had mysteriously
       disappeared two years earlier. A psychiatrist
       working on psychic knowledge, he had been writing
       a book about the odd ways people's minds can work.
       While visiting the Nancarrows, twenty-year-old Kit
       discovers a notation about a Light Maze scrawled
       across a page of the manuscript. Curious, Kit
       learns about the legend of the Light Maze and the
       Lightstone and begins to put pieces of the puzzle
       together. The problem that Kit finally solves is
       how to get into the Light Maze and return safely.

294   *Norton, Andre. <u>Octagon Magic</u>. Cleveland: World,
          1967. grades 4-6
       Coming from Canada to Ashton to live with her
       aunt, Lorrie is having problems in school--she has
       no friends, the boys taunt her, and the classes are
       different. To avoid the boys' teasing, Lorrie takes
       a shortcut through a witch's yard and discovers that

the occupants (two older women) are very friendly. In fact, Lorrie is invited back to explore the house, especially a room that contains a miniature version of the Octagon House. Through a time and space warp, Lorrie is taken into the past, where she gains personal insights that help her to face and solve her own problems.

295   *Norton, Andre. <u>Red Hart Magic</u>. New York: Crowell, 1976. grades 4+
Nan's mother and Chris's father have gotten married; however, Nan and Chris dislike each other because each is used to being the only one. While their parents are vacationing, they stay with Chris's Aunt Elizabeth. When Chris buys a miniature house and Nan discovers the way to open it, they share secret time-warp adventures from earlier English history. By testing their courage in great danger, the shared experiences help them to deal with their present-day problems.

296   *O'Daniel, Janet. <u>A Part for Addie</u>. Boston: Houghton Mifflin, 1974. grades 5+
In the 1880s, Addie and her sister Rose-Anne seek out their grandfather in Albany after their parents die. Having had small parts in traveling-theater productions and been members of The Dancing Trimbles, the girls quickly adjust to rural living. Each finds her place in an unusual household--Addie helps her grandfather to recover his health and determination after a stroke while Rose-Anne works in the house as well as in the fields. When Addie discovers a plot againt her grandfather, she finds that all of her acting and managing skills are needed to rescue him.

297   **O'Dell, Scott. <u>Sarah Bishop</u>. Boston: Houghton Mifflin, 1980. grades 7+
Because of his British sympathies during the War for Independence, Sarah's father is killed and their farm burned. Her brother leaves to join the patriot army, is captured in the first battle, and dies as a prisoner. Happening to be at the wrong place when a fire breaks out, Sarah is taken prisoner by the British but manages to escape. On her own, she discovers skills and abilities that she had not known she possessed.

298   *Orgel, Doris. The Mulberry Music. New York:
          Harper & Row, 1971. grades 4-6
       Libby, a sixth-grader, has good times with her
       grandmother, which is why she loves her so much.
       Her grandmother does "exactly what she pleases,
       how and when she pleases." She gets up early in
       the morning, goes for a swim in the pond, and then
       puts on her mulberry sweatsuit to go jogging. She
       plays the piano badly and loudly, paints, cooks, and
       gets involved in politics. But one day, Libby's
       grandmother gets sick and Libby cannot see her.
       Because of her love for her grandmother, Libby de-
       fies her parents and the hospital in order to see
       her and discovers that love and memories endure.

299   Orgel, Doris. Next Door to Xanadu. New York:
          Harper & Row, 1969. grades 4-7
       Some boys at school tease ten-year-old Patricia by
       calling her "Fatsy Patsy," and the girls just don't
       talk to her. When Dorothy moves into the next-
       door Manhattan apartment, Patricia is overjoyed,
       and they quickly become friends. Having wished so
       hard for a friend, Patsy resolves to stay away from
       snacks when her wish comes true. Dorothy helps
       Patsy get revenge on the leader of the boys who
       tease her. In addition to giving her self-confidence,
       Dorothy also shows Patsy about friendship.

300   **Paterson, Katherine. Bridge to Terabithia. New
          York: Crowell, 1977. grades 5+
       Having practiced the entire summer to become the
       fastest runner of the third, fourth, and fifth grades
       in rural Virginia, ten-year-old Jesse is upset to
       find that a new girl, Leslie, is the fastest. He
       soon discovers that Leslie is a confident, independ-
       ent, and understanding person. It is Leslie who
       shows Jess about Terabithia--their secret kingdom
       where everything seems possible. Here, together,
       they own the world. In Terabithia, Leslie learns
       compassion and compromise from Jess, and Jess
       gains strength and insight from Leslie. When Les-
       lie dies, Jess realizes that while he has lost an
       understanding friend, he must forge ahead into the
       real world for both of them.

301   **Paterson, Katherine. The Great Gilly Hopkins.
          New York: Crowell, 1978. grades 5+

Stubborn, independent, eleven-year-old Gilly is moved
from foster home to foster home because she an-
tagonizes and uses people. "Gruesome Gilly" fights
with boys, ignores girls, and tries to break her
teacher's seeming indifference because she's not used
to being treated like everyone else. Always hoping
that her real mother will come and get her, Gilly attempts several schemes but finally resorts to taking
money for a bus ticket and writing a letter to her
mother describing her situation. Gilly is stopped
before she ever gets on the bus and is returned to
her foster home. When her grandmother wants
Gilly to live with her, Gilly discovers that her
mother does not want to be responsible for her.
While Gilly learns that life is tough, she also learns
to accept love and to give it.

302   Peck, Robert Newton. Hub. New York: Knopf,
           1976. grades 3-7
       When Otto Piddle, the town's best and fastest bicy-
       clist, hurts his knee and arm a few days before the
       Chump's Landing Overland Obstacle Bicycle Race,
       someone in the town must be found to compete
       against Montana Muldoon of Setonville. Miss Guppy,
       the schoolteacher, accepts the challenge. With a
       few tricks planned to waylay Montana, Hub and
       Spooner help to increase the obstacles and help
       Miss Guppy to win the race.

303   Peck, Robert Newton. Patooie. New York: Knopf,
           1977. grades 3-7
       The champion watermelon-seed-spitter is unable to
       compete in the annual contest because of a swollen
       jaw from a toothache. A new contestant is found--
       Bertha Brimstone, the visiting bishop's wife. How-
       ever, no one is sure if she will be allowed to com-
       pete, since the rules prohibit a female contestant.
       With a little trickery, Bertha competes as Bert
       and wins the seed-spitting trophy.

304   *Peck, Robert Newton. Trig Sees Red. Boston:
           Little, Brown, 1978. grades 4-6
       When Pop the Cop, Clodsburg's only uniformed
       policeman, is replaced by a modern traffic light,
       Trig is determined to get his job back for him.
       As the leader of the Junior G-Men, Trig devises a
       plan using the mayor's bowling ball on the town's

official holiday. Trig is the first book in the series,
Trig Goes Ape is the third.

305   *Perl, Lila. Dumb Like Me, Olivia Potts. New
          York: Seabury, 1976. grades 4-6
When she has Miss Kilhenny for her fifth-grade
teacher, Olivia decides that she doesn't want to live
up to her potential or be part of the "brain chain"
that includes her older brother and sister. However, she uses her intelligence to solve the neighborhood burglaries and solve her problems with her
teacher also.

306   **Pevsner, Stella. Call Me Heller, That's My Name.
          New York: Seabury, 1973. grades 3-6
Heller (whose real name is Hildegard) is always
anxious to take dares and get into mischief. In
1927, her eleventh summer doesn't seem to be going right. Her aunt has come to take things in
hand; her sister, who has let Heller have her way,
is getting married; and her best friend, Walter
Wayne, is ignoring her to play with a new boy.
Heller is determined to show them all--she will
place lighted sparklers on her mother's grave at
midnight, regain control of her family, and show
Walter Wayne that she is as tough as any boy.
During these escapades, Heller discovers a new
meaning for courage and gains a deeper understanding of herself and others.

307   *Peyton, K.M. Fly-by-night. Cleveland: World,
          1968. grades 5-9
At twelve, Ruth knows that if she doesn't get a
pony soon she will be too big for one, and horses
definitely cost too much. Now that they have moved
from London to the country, Ruth manages to convince her father of her need. However, getting her
parents' permission is the easiest part: money for
feed, equipment, clothes, and Pony Club membership is Ruth's major concern. Ruth's inexperience
in riding, tentativeness with Fly, and lack of friends
with whom to ride also loom as significant problems
that she manages to overcome. Through determination and hard work, she makes her riding debut
in the Hunter Trials. The Team is the sequel.

308   *Pfeffer, Susan Beth. Kid Power. New York:

Watts, 1977. grades 4-6
When her mother is laid off from her job, eleven-
year-old Janie finds that she needs a way to make
money in order to buy a new bicycle. She begins
with an idea for doing odd jobs in the neighborhood,
and Kid Power is initiated. By the middle of the
summer, Kid Power is so popular it needs to be
expanded to include Janie's sister and friends while
Janie manages the agency.

309   *Pool, Eugene. The Captain of Battery Park. Read-
            ing, Mass.: Addison-Wesley, 1978. grades
            4-6
        Wanting to become an ornithologist, twelve-year-old
        Melanie goes to Battery Park to watch the birds
        across New York Harbor and keep a notebook of her
        daily observations. During a storm, she rescues an
        injured Arctic tern and meets Dr. Kidd, a veterinarian
        who helps her care for the tern. Melanie discovers
        that Dr. Kidd is planning to "liberate" young pen-
        guins from zoos so they can "regenerate their en-
        dangered species." She becomes involved in the
        project in time to sail to the Arctic with Dr. Kidd
        and the crew.

310   **Potter, Marian. Blatherskite. New York: Morrow,
            1980. grades 5+
        Living in Dotzero, Missouri, during the Depression,
        ten-year-old Maureen enjoys talking, but others call
        her "talking machine, parrot, babbling brook, and
        blatherskite." Because of her chattering, Maureen's
        teacher almost loses her job. However, Maureen
        learns that there is "a time to keep silent, and a
        time to speak" when she saves her younger brother's
        life, gives her grandmother a renewed will to live,
        brings her older brother home, and obtains a new
        bridge for the town.

311   *Potter, Marian. The Shared Room. New York:
            Morrow, 1979. grades 5+
        Ten-year-old Catherine lives with her grandparents
        because her mother is sick. Not until one of her
        school friends twirls her finger next to her temple
        does Catherine realize what kind of sick her mother
        is. Determined to know her mother, she decides
        to exercise some control over her life. Her per-
        sistence is rewarded when her mother comes home.

Although the step from institutionalization to independent home living is too large, a halfway home
is agreed to be an appropriate first step, and
Catherine succeeds in reviving hope for recovery.

312 **Rabe, Berniece. The Girl Who Had No Name.
New York: Dutton, 1977. grades 5+
After her mother's death during the Depression,
twelve-year-old Girlie is shifted from one sister
to another when her father gives her away. Girlie
has many questions about her Missouri family (what
her mother died of, why her mother is buried in the
old graveyard away from everyone else, why her
father won't let her stay with him, and why she
doesn't have a name). As she learns facts--about
herself, her parents, life--Girlie writes them in a
ledger. Her persistence eventually is rewarded
when she discovers her identity and finds a home
for herself with her father.

313 *Rabe, Berniece. Naomi. Nashville, Tenn.: Nelson, 1975. grades 7+
Living on a Missouri farm during the Depression,
eleven-year-old Naomi, who everyone says is the
spittin' image of her Aunt Wilma, doesn't want to
be a burden as her mother says Wilma was. Concerned about her future, Naomi goes to a fortune-
teller, who states that she will not live to her
fourteenth birthday. With this in mind, Naomi
sets out to "do good so God might extend her
time on earth." However, she finally becomes
disgusted with everyone's advice, decides to do
what she pleases, and chooses to become a doctor.

314 Raskin, Ellen. The Tattooed Potato and Other
Clues. New York: Dutton, 1975. grades 4-
7
Seventeen-year-old, first-year art student Dickory
Dock answers an ad for an art apprentice. She
helps Garson, the artist, solve four small mysteries
for Chief of Detectives Quinn, but Dickory solves
the more important all-encompassing mystery herself.

315 *Richard, Adrienne. Wings. Boston: Little,
Brown, 1974. grades 4+
Living in southern California in 1928, Pip dreams

of becoming an aviatrix. No one really understands
her love for airplanes or her desire to fly one except Radyar, a friend of her mother, and Harold,
a three-fingered boy in her class. With these
friends, Pip discovers that one must accept the
responsibility for personal decisions without fear
for the future, because "fear crushes life."

316 **Robertson, Keith. Henry Reed, Inc. New York:
Viking, 1958. grades 4-6
Thirteen-year-old Henry, the son of a consul sta-
tioned in Italy, has come to Princeton, New Jersey,
to spend the summer with his Aunt Mabel and Uncle
Al. Although a small town, Princeton is large
enough to support Henry Reed, Inc., a pure- and
applied-research firm. Henry and twelve-year-old
Midge agree to go into partnership when Midge con-
tributes two rabbits to the enterprise. Together,
they enter into earthworm, pigeon, oil, truffle, and
space research and discover that teamwork is a
rewarding experience. Henry Reed's Journey, Henry
Reed's Babysitting Service, and Henry Reed's Big
Show are sequels.

317 Robinson, Nancy K. Wendy and the Bullies. New
York: Hastings House, 1980. grades 3-5
Wendy, a third-grader, is afraid of bullies; however,
she has a system for dealing with the Class A, B,
and C bullies. A map in her Bully Command Post
shows where each bully lives and his classification.
When her best friend is sick all week, Wendy has
a problem. She tries to be "sick" all week, but
that plan fails. Suddenly, Wendy finds herself
speaking up. She discovers that she has a common
interest with a Class A bully and that her Bully Command Post system can be useful in solving another
problem.

318 Sachs, Marilyn. Amy Moves In. Garden City,
N.Y.: Doubleday, 1964. grades 4-7
Nine-year-old Amy and her older sister Laura are
faced with the problem of making new friends when
they move. Amy's habit of lying eventually gets
in her way with her friends, but she overcomes this
to accept Rosa, who has not been accepted by her
classmates. Amy's best friend sways Amy's o-
pinions of Rosa; however, Amy finally decides to

hold her own opinions no matter what the consequences.

319   *Sachs, Marilyn. <u>A December Tale</u>. Garden City,
            N. Y.: Doubleday, 1976. grades 5-9
        Ten-year-old Myra and her brother Henry, six
        years old, live in a foster home because their
        father and his wife don't want to take care of them.
        Henry doesn't behave or mind anyone. Myra, being
        his sister, is supposed to be able to deal with him.
        While Mrs. Smith, their foster mother, deals with
        Henry by beating him, Myra tries to deal with
        reality by imagining that she is Joan of Arc. How-
        ever, when the beatings become severe, Myra must
        face reality and deal with the situation herself.

320   Sachs, Marilyn. <u>Dorrie's Book</u>. Garden City,
            N. Y.: Doubleday, 1975. grades 4-7
        When her English teacher hands out copies of The
        Tales of King Arthur as a class assignment, eleven-
        year-old Dorrie states that it isn't relevant. There-
        fore, the teacher gives the class a choice of writing
        their own books or reading the assignment. Dorrie
        chooses to write a book (this story) about her ex-
        periences when her mother has triplets and her
        parents become foster parents.

321   *Sachs, Marilyn. <u>Veronica Ganz.</u> Garden City,
            N. Y.: Doubleday, 1968. grades 4-7
        Veronica, who is in the eighth grade, is the biggest
        one in her class. She bullies everyone, even those
        her five-year-old brother's age, because no one
        ever takes her part. But Veronica can't seem to
        "take care of" the new kid, Peter Wedemeyer, who
        keeps tormenting her with jingles, laughing at her,
        and playing tricks on her. When Veronica thinks
        she has a foolproof plan to get Peter, it fails as
        Peter and two friends successfully beat her at her
        own game. However, Veronica discovers that Peter
        is the one person she likes and admires the most.
        She knows that this is just the beginning of a friend-
        ship. <u>Peter and Veronica</u> is the sequel.

322   **St. George, Judith. <u>The Chinese Puzzle of Shag
            Island.</u> New York: Putnam, 1976. grades
            5-8
        Thirteen-year-old Kim and her mother go to Shag

Island to visit Kim's great-grandfather and to pre-
pare his house for sale. During Kim's first days
at The Anchorage, she hears Chinese music, watches
the housekeeper pocket mail, sees a young boy hiding on the island, finds a secret panel containing her
great-great-grandfather's old letters and diaries,
and observes her great-grandfather's strange behavior. Realizing that her great-grandfather is in
danger, Kim solves the mystery of Shag Island.

323   *St. John, Wylly Folk. The Mystery Book Mystery.
       New York: Viking, 1976. grades 5-9
       When seventeen-year-old Libby Clark registers for
       a Writers' Conference, she doesn't know that she
       will become involved in a real-life murder mystery.
       Wanting to base her fictional mystery on the real-
       life murder on campus, Libby delves into the back-
       grounds of the Writers' Conference participants,
       puts the pieces together, and solves the murder.

324   *Sargent, Shirley. Stop the Typewriters. New York:
       Abelard-Schuman, 1963. grades 4-7
       Nancy and her friends--Sam, Cleo, and Howie--need
       a way to earn money since each one has his or her
       own special project. Having tried many other
       money-making schemes (carnivals, plays, and sell-
       ing flowers), Nancy, who wants to become a writer,
       suggests writing a local newspaper. The paper is
       successful, and while they gather news, the group
       finds they are in the middle of a local land-grabbing
       scheme.

325   *Sarton, May. As We Are Now. New York: Norton,
       1973. grades 9+
       Caro, a former teacher, is forced to live in a re-
       mote nursing home, where her rapidly declining
       pride and self-respect lead her to commit a tragic
       act.

326   *Selfridge, Oliver G. Trouble with Dragons. Read-
       ing, Mass.: Addison-Wesley, 1978. grades
       5-9
       Three sisters set out to find and marry princes.
       However, before a prince and princess can live
       happily ever after, the princess has to perform a
       difficult task--slay a dragon. Two of the princesses
       leave to slay the dragon but are eaten. The third

princess, who is more cautious and clever, succeeds in slaying the dragon and marrying her prince.

327   *Sharmat, Marjorie Weinman. Getting Something on Maggie Marmelstein. New York: Harper & Row, 1971. grades 4-6
When Thad calls Maggie a mouse, Maggie retaliates by calling him Thaddeus Gideon Smith (his real name, which he has tried to keep a secret). Now, the battle is on. Maggie discovers some information about Thad that he doesn't want everyone to know, but she waits for the right moment with the largest audience. Thad realizes that he must stop her by GSOMMM (Getting Something on Mouse Maggie Marmelstein). He finally uncovers a secret about Maggie, and they discover that there is a fine line between Enemy and Friend. Maggie Marmelstein for President is the sequel.

328   *Slaatten, Evelyn. The Good, the Bad, and the Rest of Us. New York: Morrow, 1980. grades 3-7
Living in the 1930s during the Depression, ten-year-old Katie feels it is unfair that the Featherstones are rich while her family is poor. Her mother insists that "money isn't everything," but Katie isn't sure of this fact until she finds that the Featherstones have other problems--a father who drinks, a lack of love and family cohesiveness, and a critically injured son. During her father's unemployment and her friend's hospitalization, Katie makes many wishes and says many prayers. However, when her friend is better and her father has a job, Katie discovers that she has everything.

329   **Smith, Doris Buchanan. Dreams & Drummers. New York: Crowell, 1978. grades 6+
First-chair drummer in the junior high band, fourteen-year-old Stephanie can't decide what she wants to become when there are so many things she likes to do. Beginning to question her beliefs and behavior, Stephanie must respond to excitement and experiences--having a boy for a friend, bicycling over a distance, losing her first chair in the drum section, losing the science-fair exhibition, admiring a friend's independence, and appreciating her own family relationships. Stephanie realizes

that she wants to continue experiencing new situations and relationships but without compromising herself.

330   **Smith, Doris Buchanan. <u>Kick a Stone Home.</u> New
          York: Crowell, 1974. grades 5+
      A shy fifteen-year-old girl who wants to be a veterinarian, Sara feels more at home on the football, basketball, or baseball field than she does at school, at home, or with others. Tentatively, she begins to seek friends--boys, young married couples, teachers, her mother and father (who are divorced), and even her father's wife--gains more self-confidence, and finds it easier to be herself.

331   **Smith, Doris Buchanan. <u>Salted Lemons.</u> New
          York: Four Winds, 1980. grades 5+
      Having moved from Washington, D.C., to Atlanta during World War II, ten-year-old Darby finds it difficult to adjust to her new environment. The language, culture, and people are different from what she is accustomed to. Even though Darby knows that names cannot hurt her, she is confused when the neighborhood children call her a Yankee and a Jap lover. When her friends are called a spy and a Jap, Darby even begins to wonder about them. However, she learns to accept the bad with the good and finds friendship.

332   **Snyder, Zilpha Keatley. <u>And All Between.</u> New
          York: Atheneum, 1976. grades 5-8
      Life in the underground caves of Erda had not always been one of hunger. But with too many Erdling people and too little food in the caves, even eight-year-old Teera's pet is needed for food. At this pronouncement, Teera flees with her pet and escapes to Green-sky through the deteriorating root that holds them captive. Taken in by a Kindar family, Teera is curious about this different way of life and shares her information about Erda with Pomma, the girl in the family. However, this information puts them in danger, and they are taken prisoner by the Geets-kel, the governing body of the Kindar people. In determining the girls' fate and ultimately the fate of the Kindar and Erdling people, the wisdom of a child's nonsense song is recalled: "What is the answer? When will it come? When all between be-

comes among, ... And all is one...." Below the
Root is the first volume in this science-fiction fanta-
sy.

333   **Snyder, Zilpha Keatley. The Changeling. New
        York: Atheneum, 1972. grades 5-8
As a child, Martha earned the nickname of Marty
Mouse at home because of her shyness and inse-
curity. However, over eight years, Marty discovers some special talents of her own--acting and
writing--as well as self-confidence and courage
through Ivy. Ivy, who has boundless confidence,
spirit, and imagination, explains her uniqueness by
declaring that she is a changeling. As the girls
create an imaginary kingdom, they find that they
enjoy playing by their own rules. When Ivy decides at thirteen that she doesn't want to grow up,
she invents a spell to prevent her from becoming
an adult. At sixteen, Marty finds that she can
determine who she is and what she wants to do--
to be unique--because of Ivy's example and friendship.

334   **Snyder, Zilpha Keatley. The Egypt Game. New
        York: Atheneum, 1967. grades 3-7
Eleven-year-old April has moved in with her grandmother. Being inquisitive, she explores her neighborhood and visits the Professor's second-hand
store. With a neighbor girl and her younger brother,
April discovers a loose board in the Professor's
backyard fence. In the yard is a bust of Nefertiti,
a broken birdbath, a small lean-to, and some
pillars--which are the beginnings for the complex
Egypt Game that evolves through the girls' crea-
tivity. Eventually, a couple of the sixth-grade boys
become involved in the development of the Egypt
Game also.

335   **Snyder, Zilpha Keatley. The Truth About Stone
        Hollow. New York: Atheneum, 1975. grades
        4-6
Stone Hollow is the local haunted place, but no one
(not even the school bully) dares to go there. Amy
is curious, but it isn't until a new boy, Jason, offers to take her there that she has the courage to
go. Jason is crazy, according to Amy and the
rest of the sixth-graders. He doesn't fight or tease

back when he is attacked; he has a large vocabulary; but his behavior is sometimes immature. While Amy helps Jason covertly, he shows her that there are different kinds of courage and truth.

336 *Sobol, Donald. Greta the Strong. Chicago: Follett, 1970. grades 3-7
After King Arthur's Round Table is dissolved, violence runs rampant. Seeking a new hero, the last of the knights arrives at a farm, where four sons compete for the honor of the knighthood. However, their younger sister Greta bests them and is given the honor. Despite her brothers' trickery, a sorcerer, a dragon, other evils, and her True Love, Greta is able to fulfill her quest in her own way.

337 Sortor, Toni. Adventures of B.J.: The Amateur Detective. Nashville, Tenn.: Abingdon, 1975. grades 3-6
Eleven-year-old B.J. discovers that an organized group of school-age children are shoplifting and fencing items from a department store. However, in order to resolve the thefts, B.J. must determine and catch the leader of the shoplifting ring.

338 **Speare, Elizabeth George. The Witch of Blackbird Pond. Boston: Houghton Mifflin, 1958. grades 7+
Having lived with her grandfather in Barbados in comparative wealth all of her sixteen years, Kit is unprepared for the plainness of America. When her grandfather dies, Kit sails alone to her only relatives, an aunt and her family in Connecticut. An impulsive and independent person, Kit faces many problems in dealing with the different customs and lifestyle of the Puritans. When she meets the witch of Blackbird Pond, she finds an answer to her frustrations--be determined to keep on trying.

339 *Spykman, E.C. Edie On the Warpath. New York: Harcourt, Brace & World, 1966. grades 5-9
Edie is eleven in 1913. Planning for the future, Edie decides to help the suffragists in the hope that they will vote for her when she runs for President. She proposes to join a parade for suffrage and convinces her friend, Fatty McHenry to dress as a girl. Even before they reach the parade, Fatty and

Edie are approached by a policemen, who wants to take them to the station. While Fatty leads the parade, Edie is taken to the police station, where her father must explain her behavior. Other adventures await the energetic, irrepressible Edie. This is the sequel to A Lemon and a Star and Terrible, Horrible Edie.

340   *Storr, Catherine. Lucy Runs Away. Englewood Cliffs, N.J.: Prentice-Hall, 1969. grades 2-5
Wanting to have adventures, Lucy tells her family that she is going to run away when she is ten years old. At ten, imagining herself to be the Mysterious Outlaw, Lucy leaves London for Haven by the sea. Lucy finds her adventures when she saves a drowning man. A hero, she is returned to her family in London, where she promises not to run away until she is twelve.

341   **Stoutenberg, Adrien. Where to Now, Blue? New York: Four Winds, 1978. grades 3-7
Twelve-year-old Blueberry feels there is nothing for her in Chicksaw Landing, Minnesota--especially since her older brother ran away--so she is running away herself. She plans to sail down the Mississippi to her Uncle Stewart in Minneapolis. Reluctantly, Blue finds herself with a companion, six-year-old Tibo from the orphanage. Confronted with several problems, Blue and Tibo finally reach Minneapolis to find that her uncle has died and her aunt is unable to take care of them. Undaunted, Blue declares that "a person has to keep hanging onto a dream, or find a new one, when the first one smashes." Blue and Tibo return home having learned more about themselves, their abilities, friendship, and plans for the future.

342   *Streatfeild, Noel. Ballet Shoes. New York: Random House, 1937. grades 4-7
Great-uncle Matthew, an eccentric and famous London fossil-hunter, finds and adopts three baby girls. Leaving them with his great-niece and her nurse, Gum (Great-uncle Matthew) sets sail for some strange islands. As the girls grow, Gum's money diminishes, and it is decided to take in boarders. In 1936 the girls are sent to an academy of

dancing and stage training so they can earn money.
The girls find that one has a talent for acting,
another for dancing, and the other for flying and
being a car mechanic.

343   *Symons, Geraldine. <u>Crocuses Were Over, Hitler
         Was Dead</u>. Philadelphia: Lippincott, 1977.
         grades 5+
Jassy visits her grandmother's former cook and
gardener at an old English manor that is being restored. During her first exploration of the estate,
she sees someone fishing by the bridge, but when
she investigates further, she finds that he has
disappeared. Later, when she speaks with the
mysterious man, Jassy discovers that she is in a
time warp between two worlds--one at the start of
World War II, the other many years later. Curious
to learn about the former inhabitants of the manor,
Jassy continues to explore and seek out her friend,
only to discover that he was a soldier killed during
World War II.

344   *Symons, Geraldine. <u>Miss Rivers and Miss Bridges</u>.
         New York: Macmillan, 1971. grades 6-8
When thirteen-year-old Pansy visits Atalanta in
London at the turn of the century, she is not pre-
pared for her friend's protest activities for the
WSPU (Women's Social and Political Union). Dis-
guising themselves as the matronly suffragists Miss
Rivers and Miss Bridges, they smash a window of
the Prime Minister's house and disrupt a play, for
which they are taken to jail. However, their jail
term is short, since their identities are revealed
when Atalanta's mother arrives to have them re-
leased. This is the sequel to <u>The Workhouse
Child</u>.

345   **Tave, Isabella. <u>Not Bad for a Girl</u>. New York:
         Evans, 1972. grades 5+
When twelve-year-old Sharon is finally given the
opportunity to play on a local Little League team,
she is thrilled by the challenge of the situation but
unprepared for the threats, hatred, and problems
generated by her participation. However, Sharon
steadfastly confronts the pressures and continues
to participate on the team until the team manager
is dismissed. This book is based on an actual inci-
dent that received national publicity.

346   *Terris, Susan. <u>Tucker and the Horse Thief</u>. New
          York: Four Winds, 1979. grades 7+
       Accompanying her father to the California gold
       fields in 1856, twelve-year-old Tucker is disguised
       as a boy to protect herself from the dangers of the
       uncivilized West.   Since she is lonely, Tucker is
       happy to find a friend in thirteen-year-old Solomon
       Weil.   However, Tucker knows she cannot be close
       to him since he thinks she is a boy.   When Tucker
       begins to realize that she has to take care of her-
       self, she decides to run away to San Francisco with
       Sol.   However, before they can leave, Tucker's
       father is killed, which prompts Tucker to consider
       asking her mother and family to join her in Califor-
       nia.   Although Sol is angry and disappointed to learn
       that Tucker is female, they depart friends.

347   *Thompson, Wilma. <u>That Barbara!</u> New York:
          Dell, 1969. grades 4-7
       It seems that Barbara's mother is always saying,
       "Won't you ever learn to stop and consider?" Being
       thirteen, going on fourteen, in 1925, Barbara be-
       gins to feel the pressures of growing up and, like
       her mother, wonders if she will ever be responsible.
       As she tries to prove herself and earn the necklace
       of her brave ancestor, the first Barbara, Barbara
       impulsively engages in hilarious misadventures.
       However, when Barbara very ably cares for her
       sick nephew alone during a severe rainstorm, her
       mother decides that Barbara has grown up enough
       to receive the first Barbara's necklace.

348   **Tolan, Stephanie S. <u>The Liberation of Tansy War-</u>
          <u>ner.</u> New York: Scribner, 1980. grades 6+
       Having won the lead in the school play, Tansy (a
       ninth-grader) hopes that her father will recognize
       her achievement.   Rushing home to share the news
       with her mother, who has encouraged her acting,
       Tansy discovers the note from her mother stating
       that she has left to find some value in the world.
       Although she finds her mother, Tansy learns that
       she must discover her place in life by herself.

349   **Tolle, Jean Bashor. <u>The Great Pete Penney.</u>
          New York: Atheneum, 1979. grades 3-7
       Eleven-year-old Priscilla "Pete" Penney is the only
       girl on the Blue Sox major/minor Little League

team. One Saturday before baseball season, Pete
meets Mike McGlory, a leprechaun, who allows her
one wish. She wishes to pitch for her baseball
team and have a really good curve ball. Mike
places an invisible ring on her little finger, which
she can use when she wants to throw a curve ball.
With Mike's coaching and the magic ring, Pete is
asked to join a major team as a pitcher. After
the team wins the pennant, Pete has a fight with
Mike McGlory, and he takes back the ring. Pete
worries about losing Mike's friendship and support,
but discovers that she doesn't really need the ring.

350   Van Leeuwen, Jean.   I Was a 98-Pound Duckling.
       New York: Dial, 1972.   grades 7+
Being thirteen, weighing ninety-eight pounds, and
having problems, Kathy feels that nothing is ever
going to happen to her in her entire life. Although
she fantasizes about her future as an architect, she
wonders whether she will really be anything other
than an ugly duckling. Kathy has read all the beauty
books about how to act and what to say, but when
she meets Keith she decides to be herself and finds
that to be the best solution. However, even though
her life has changed drastically in some ways, Kathy
discovers that in other ways her life has not changed
at all.

351   **Vining, Elizabeth Gray.   The Taken Girl.   New
       York: Viking, 1972.   grades 7+
Veer, a fifteen-year-old orphan, becomes a part
of the Underwood household as a "taken girl" (servant) and is told that she must "see cake and want
cake and not eat cake." When that situation does
not work out, Mrs. Healy offers her a position in
her Quaker household, where she becomes involved
in making clothes for runaway slaves and helping
to publish an abolitionist newspaper in pre-Civil
War Philadelphia.

352   Walden, Amelia Elizabeth.   My Sister Mike.   New
       York: Berkley, 1956.   grades 4-8
Mike, a senior in high school, is a good basketball
player. Unlike her younger sister, Mike is not
popular or beautiful, but she doesn't envy her sister.
After one of her basketball games, a boy she likes
asks her for a date. When she finds out that her

date is an initiation for him, she decides to make the best of it, have a good time, and be herself.

353   Waldron, Ann.   The Integration of Mary Larkin
         Thornhill.   New York: Dutton, 1975.   grades
         5+
Mary Larkin and Critter Kingsley are almost the only white students at newly integrated Wheatley Junior High, and Mary thinks she'd rather die. Her friends move or lie about their addresses in order to attend the white junior high, but her mother and father (the Presbyterian minister) will not let her change schools. When her white friends call her names and almost force her family out of the church, Mary Larkin discovers that she belongs at Wheatley.

354   *Wallace, Barbara Brooks.   Peppermints in the Par-
         lor.   New York: Atheneum, 1980.   grades 4-
         6
When her parents die, eleven-year-old Emily is sent to live with her Aunt and Uncle Twice in San Francisco. Emily fondly remembers Sugar Hill Hall, their home. However, when she arrives, she discovers that her aunt is terrified of tyrannical Mrs. Meeching, who is running Sugar Hill Hall as a retirement home; her uncle seems to have disappeared; and Emily is expected to work as a servant. Emily is determined to find some answers and succeeds in her task.

355   *Wallace, Barbara Brooks.   The Secret Summer of
         L. E. B.   Chicago: Follett, 1974.   grades 4-6
When Lizabeth moves to a new school, she somehow becomes a member of the VIGs and Bs--the Very Important Girls and Boys--of the sixth grade. In order to be part of the group, Lizabeth sometimes has to say and do things she doesn't like. When she discovers an old house--her secret house--she also finds CD, Creepy Douglas, the class outcast. Lizabeth soon discovers that she likes Loren (CD's real name) and can't enjoy the secret house without him. They agree to be secret friends. However, Lizabeth learns that there are different kinds of friendship and that any friendship is complicated and risky.

356   *Wallace, Barbara Brooks.   Victoria.   Chicago:

Follett, 1972. grades 4-7
Victoria and Dilys are eleven years old, but Dilys
finds herself always trying to be Victoria's friend
and gain her approval. The two girls discover that
they will be going to the same private school. They
and their roommates establish a secret group, the
Victorians, with Victoria as their leader and the
Black Book as their guide to ward off "evil forces."
When Dilys becomes upset with Victoria's unreason-
able demands, she rebels against her leadership,
until she learns the truth and gains a new understanding of friendship.

357   **Watson, Sally. Highland Rebel. New York: Holt,
          Rinehart & Winston, 1954. grades 4-7
When Prince Charles returns to Scotland in 1745
to claim the English throne, eleven-year-old Lauren
is upset that she, as a young lass, will not be able
to join in the fighting. Wearing kilts, fencing, and
practicing with a wooden claymore, Lauren states
that she wouldn't mind being a lass if she could do
all the things lads do. So, Lauren and her cousins,
Dugald and Janet, scout for spies and find a way to
help "bonny Prince Charles."

358   **Watson, Sally. The Hornet's Nest. New York:
          Holt, Rinehart & Winston, 1968. grades
          5-8
When an American cousin comes to Scotland in
1773 to trace the family genealogy, he discovers
that fourteen-year-old Lauchlin and her brother
Ronald are anxious to do all they can to defy British rule. Together, they decide to write, illus-
trate, and publish a newspaper informing the Scottish and British citizens of the colonies' quarrel
with King George. When Ronald and Lauchlin are
sent to America to keep out of trouble, they send
articles and illustrations to their cousin in Scotland
about the pre-Revolutionary War happenings.

359   **Watson, Sally. Jade. New York: Holt, Rinehart
          & Winston, 1969. grades 5-8
Living in the 1700s, sixteen-year-old Jade is "no
lady at all. She has no sense of propriety or
shame or family dignity; her pride is entirely the
wrong sort; even her virtues of courage and honesty
are altogether willful and reckless." Her father

and family can't understand her at all and are unable to handle her. Since Jade despises slavery,
she releases a cargo of slaves on a ship and is
caught and whipped. At that moment the slaver is
attacked by the female pirate Anne Bonney, who
rescues Jade. Later, Jade voluntarily joins the
pirate crew.

360   **Watson, Sally. Linnet. New York: Dutton, 1971.
           grades 5-7
       An impish girl, fourteen-year-old Linnet runs away
       from her godparents' home in 1582 to have an ad-
       venture in London. She meets Sir Colin, who volun-
       teers to give her a ride. Arriving in London, she
       finds that she has been taken prisoner by the Up-
       right Man, the master of the underworld. He "con-
       vinces" Linnet to aid him in spying on the Papists,
       who are plotting to overthrow Queen Elizabeth. By
       her independent spirit, Linnet creates some problems
       for Colley while helping him, but she also begins
       to look upon her colleagues as people and to gain
       their friendship. When her friend Giles arrives
       to "rescue" her from Colley, he requires both Lin-
       net's and her friends' help to escape and warn the
       Secretary of State of the plot to overthrow the Queen.

361   *Watson, Sally. Magic at Wychwood. New York:
           Knopf, 1970. grades 4-7
       Unlike typical princesses, Elaine is known as "a
       proper little wildfire" by the townspeople. When
       the royal tutor refuses to acknowledge magic, Elaine
       is determined to prove its existence. She acquires
       a Thing That Goes Bump in the Night, a squire is
       changed into a pair of boots, and a wicked fairy at-
       tends a christening to cast spells on everyone. How-
       ever, it isn't until the professor accidentally casts
       a spell on his favorite chair that he acquiesces on
       the subject of magic--but he prefers to call it "ap-
       plied science."

362   **Watson, Sally. Mistress Malapert. New York:
           Holt, 1955. grades 7-9
       Since her parents have been commanded by Queen
       Elizabeth in 1599 to go on a diplomatic mission to
       France, thirteen-year-old Valerie must stay with
       an aunt and uncle who vow to make her behave.
       However, disguised as a boy, Valerie runs away to

become a player with a traveling theater troupe.
When she is offered a chance to act with the Shake-
speare company, she accepts. It isn't until she
plays before Queen Elizabeth that she is discovered
to be a girl, and the Queen commands her to return
home.

363   *Whitney, Phyllis A. Mystery of the Strange Traveler.
          Philadelphia: Westminster, 1951. grades 4-
          6
       Thirteen-year-old Laurie and fourteen-year-old
       Celia go to Staten Island to live with their aunt.
       There they discover the identity of a family ancestor
       and the ghost image of a stagecoach.

364   Whitney, Phyllis A. Secret of the Emerald Star.
          Philadelphia: Westminster, 1964. grades 5-9
       Thirteen-year-old Robin decides that she wants to
       take private lessons from a famous sculptor. How-
       ever, her parents are skeptical of her interest.
       She sets herself a high goal when she decides to do
       a bust of Stella, the blind girl next door. Wishing
       to protect her, Stella's grandmother does not like
       the idea of Stella posing. The grandmother's cold-
       ness, Stella's inconsistent behavior, a mysterious
       man watching Robin, an emerald-star pin, and
       talk of guns are confusing to Robin until she solves
       the mystery.

365   *Williams, Barbara. Where Are You, Angela von
          Hauptmann, Now That I Need You? New
          York: Holt, Rinehart & Winston, 1979.
          grades 5-9
       A very talkative, assertive, concerned, and self-
       confident Angela moves into the seventh grade at
       Walt Whitman Elementary in the spring of 1939.
       Her unusual behavior affects everyone. Being per-
       suasive, Angela convinces a teacher to schedule the
       traditional Field Day, coaches Ben to sprint and
       throw the discus, discusses cleanliness with Madeline
       and helps others to see her as a person, and teaches
       Woody that he can do anything as soon as he gets
       his serendipity.

366   *Williams, Ursula Moray. The Cruise of the Happy-
          Go-Gay. New York: Meredith, 1967. grades
          3-6

Bored because they can't have any fun, Aunt
Hegarty's five nieces are delighted when she invites
them to her house for adventure. They buy a steam-
ship, learn to operate it, and set sail on a voyage
of discovery. Out on the high seas, they encounter
two young male stowaways, a storm, pirates, and island natives, but they competently deal with each
situation to return home safely.

367   Winthrop, Elizabeth. <u>Marathon Miranda</u>. New
            York: Holiday House, 1979. grades 4-6
When it seems as if she is being left out of everyone's life, Miranda meets Phoebe, an enthusiastic
jogger. Phoebe convinces Miranda that jogging
would give her greater lung capacity. Despite being
afraid of an asthma attack, Miranda enters a marathon with Phoebe, and they both finish. <u>Miranda
in the Middle</u> is the sequel.

368   Yolen, Jane. <u>Shirlick Holmes and the Case of the
            Wandering Wardrobe</u>. New York: Coward,
            McCann & Geoghegan, 1981. grades 4-7
Shirli wants to be a famous detective when she grows
up. With four friends, she decides to investigate
cases involving antique furniture stolen from summer
houses. When Shirli is accidentally kidnapped by the
thieves at a stake-out, the group helps to solve the
cases and capture the thieves.

369   *Yolen, Jane. <u>The Transfigured Hart</u>. New York:
            Crowell, 1975. grades 4+
Although twelve-year-old Richard is a loner and
Heather is an "enjoyer," they find that they have
much in common. Mostly, they share the secret
of an albino deer (hart), which they believe to be
a unicorn. Together, Heather and Richard make
plans to tame the deer, but their plan is forgotten
when each thinks the other is undependable. Realizing that it is the last opportunity to save the deer
before the opening of the hunting season, both
Heather and Richard go to the forest alone. When
each sees the other, they forgive each other as
they unite to save the deer. Miraculously, the
deer comes to them and "what was logical and what
was magical became one."

370   **Young, Miriam. <u>No Place for Mitty</u>. New York:

Four Winds, 1976. grades 4-6
Always energetic, ten-year-old Mitty plays on the
girls' baseball team and with her two older brothers
in San Francisco in the late 1800s. However, when
her parents get a divorce, Mitty is sent to live in
Oakland with her Aunty Bowman and her husband
because they can better provide for her. Although
difficult for a girl who wants to be a circus performer, a baseball player, or a sulky driver, Mitty
behaves "like a lady" so she can visit her family
on her grandparents' farm. When Mitty has lived
with her aunt and uncle a year and a half, her
grandparents miss her and come to visit. Learning
the stifling conditions under which Mitty lives, her
grandmother decides that Mitty must return to the
farm with them. This news thrills Mitty, since
now she feels she has a place in her family.

371   **Zistel, Era. Good Companions. Boston: Little,
         Brown, 1980. grades 6+
Having moved from New York to the Catskills, Era
finds that animals--especially a cat, chipmunk, and
goats--make good companions. From "conferences"
with Squeak the cat, she learns how to relax--"how
to accept, and endure, and then enjoy, with no
thought of yesterday or tomorrow." The animals
give Era a "treasure box full of memories"--Squeak's
first tentative friendship to his routine "conferences, "
a goat's struggle to overcome two strokes, and a
chipmunk's bold advances for attention. However,
the author must also reflect on the proper perspective of living things and the cycle of life and death.

372   *Bryan, Ashley. <u>The Dancing Granny.</u> New York:
         Atheneum, 1977. grades K-3
       Whatever Granny does, she dances to it. She
       dances morning, noon, and night, and even in her
       dreams. Spider Ananse doesn't work or dance,
       but by singing a song, he starts Granny dancing so
       he can steal the vegetables in her garden. How-
       ever, he finally has to pay for his tricks when
       Granny forces him to dance with her.

373   *Clifton, Lucille. <u>Everett Anderson's Friend.</u> New
         York: Holt, Rinehart & Winston, 1976. grades
         K-3
       Anxiously awaiting the arrival of the new neighbors,
       Everett is disappointed when the family consists of
       girls. However, when Everett is locked out of his
       apartment, Maria invites him to wait for his mother
       in their apartment, and Everett finds that Maria and
       her family are "a lovely surprise." In addition,
       Maria, "who wins at ball, is fun to play with after
       all."

374   *Fenner, Carol. <u>The Skates of Uncle Richard.</u>
         New York: Random House, 1978. grades 2-
         5
       Nine-year-old Marsha imagines herself to be a
       graceful, beautiful skating champion. She "prac-
       tices" skating in the living room and critically
       watches the skaters on television. However, she
       doesn't own a pair of skates. For Christmas,
       Marsha finally receives a pair, but they are her
       Uncle Richard's old ugly black hockey skates.

Disappointed, she puts them in her closet for several weeks, but she finally gets them out to try her luck. She is a terrible skater, but with Uncle Richard's help, Marsha improves.

375 **Mayer, Mercer. Liza Lou and the Yeller Belly Swamp. New York: Parents' Magazine, 1976. grades K-5
Liza Lou is able to outsmart the swamp haunt, witch, slithery gobblygook, and devil from the Yeller Belly Swamp when she visits her grandmother.

376 Udry, Janice May. Mary Jo's Grandmother. Chicago: Whitman, 1970. grades K-3
Mary Jo's grandmother lives alone in the country without a telephone. When Mary Jo stays with her during Christmas vacation, she walks through the snow for help after her grandmother falls and is unable to get up.

377 *Welber, Robert. The Train. New York: Pantheon, 1972. grades K-3
Elizabeth especially enjoys seeing the train as it goes past her home. When everyone in the family is too busy to take her across the meadow to see the train, they encourage her to try it alone. Afraid of what is in the long grass, Elizabeth sits on the window seat for days watching the train go by. Early one morning, Elizabeth overcomes her fear, decides to cross the meadow alone, and finds that it isn't so scary.

---

378 **Clifford, Mary Louise. Bisha of Burundi. New
York: Crowell, 1973. grades 5+
Fifteen-year-old Bisha is a Tutsi and granddaughter
of the government-appointed headman. Nearing the
end of her sixth year of school in the late 1960s,
Bisha asks the Belgian nuns to apply for a scholar-
ship for her so she can continue her education to
become a teacher. However, at the same time,
her parents are arranging her marriage to an older,
widowed government official with three children.
When Bisha realizes that she does not want to marry
the government official and instead wants to receive
a teacher's certificate, she finds a way to inform
her parents of her decision.

379 **Coolidge, Olivia. Come by Here. Boston: Houghton Mifflin, 1970. grades 5+
Living in Baltimore in the early 1900s, seven-year-
old Minty Lou is comfortable and innocent as an
only child. Her father is a blue-collar worker, and
her mother has a good job at the hospital as the
kitchen supervisor. However, when her parents are
killed, Minty Lou learns about being poor, being a
pawn for adults who are either cruel or indifferent,
and having initiative. From the outset, Minty Lou
is adamant in her fight for self-determination and
dignity.

380 **Fitzhugh, Louise. Nobody's Family Is Going to
Change. New York: Farrar, Straus & Giroux,
1974. grades 5-9
Emma, eleven years old, wants to become a lawyer.

Although her father is an assistant district attorney, he laughs at the idea of his daughter in the courtroom. Emma's mother thinks that she should think about marrying a lawyer and raising two charming children. Emma's seven-year-old brother is having a similar problem. He shows a talent for dancing and wants to become a dancer, but his father wants him to become a lawyer. Emma finally gains insight into their problem ("nobody's family is going to change") and takes matters into her own hands.

381   **Greene, Bette. Philip Hall Likes Me. I Reckon
          Maybe. New York: Dial, 1974. grades 3-6
       Philip Hall is the best in every subject in his class.
       Eleven-year-old Beth doesn't mind being second
       best, but she wonders if she is letting him be best.
       She decides that she wants to be Randolph County's
       first veterinarian and sets up a vegetable stand with
       "a friend" (Philip Hall) to earn some money for
       college. When Beth decides to do her best to beat
       him in the calf-raising contest for the county fair,
       she succeeds and learns that Philip Hall "sometimes
       reckons he likes her" anyway. The sequel is Get
       On Out of Here, Philip Hall.

382   *Greenfield, Eloise. Sister. New York: Crowell
          Co., 1974. grades 5-12
       People always said that thirteen-year-old Doretha
       ("Sister") looked like her older sister, Alberta,
       and at times that was all right. But as Alberta
       gets older (about sixteen) and after their father
       dies, Sister does not want to be like Alberta, who
       has turned inward and will not let her feelings show
       so she can't be hurt. Sister decides that although
       she and Alberta may look alike, they are different
       people and do not have to end up the same way.

383   *Guy, Rosa. Edith Jackson. New York: Viking,
          1978. grades 8+
       A seventeen-year-old teenager tries valiantly to
       keep her family together but sees her world collapse
       as her younger sisters reject her inept mothering.
       Edith finally discovers that it is up to her to decide
       and shape her own future.

384   **Haynes, Betsy. Cowslip. Nashville, Tenn.: Nel-
          son, 1973. grades 6+

In 1861, thirteen-year-old Cowslip is on the auction
block. On the eve of her arrival at her new master's plantation, several slaves escape, and Cowslip
questions their motive, since she had been told by
a preacher that it is the Lord's will that there be
slaves. When Job, who was a freed slave, offers
to teach Cowslip to read and write (which is against
the law), Cowslip is skeptical. However, after one
of her friends is shot in an escape attempt, she
decides to accept Job's offer so at least her mind
can be free. When another escape fails, Cowslip
asserts her human dignity and is determined to be
"wild and free. "

385   **Howard, Moses L. The Ostrich Chase. New York:
        Holt, Rinehart & Winston, 1974. grades 4-8
Khuana is an adolescent Bushman living in the
Kalahari desert in Africa. She wants to hunt like
the boys and men, but tribal laws forbid it to girls
and women. Khuana's greatest dream is to hunt
an ostrich to get an eggshell for a canteen and
beads. When the group is forced to move from
lack of food and water, Khuana's grandmother must
stay behind in the desert since she cannot keep up.
Khuana returns to her grandmother, and with their
combined skills, they are able to defeat the "angry
desert, " and Khuana achieves her dream of an ostrich egg.

386   **Hurmence, Belinda. Tough Tiffany. Garden City,
        N. Y. : Doubleday, 1980. grades 7+
Eleven-year-old Tiffany Cox writes that she is
"tall and tough. " She's tough because she wants to
help her fifteen-year-old unmarried half-sister return to being happy, the way she was before she
got pregnant. Tiffany is tough because she finds
a way to pay for the bunk beds and dressers in
the girls' room. Also, Tiffany is tough since she
is the only one who can stand up to her grandmother's scolding and stinginess.

387   Jackson, Jesse. Tessie. New York: Harper &
        Row, 1968. grades 3-8
When Tessie, a ninth-grader, is given a scholar-
ship to attend a private white school on Fifth Ave-
nue, she doesn't know all the problems she will
have to face and solve both at home in Harlem and
at school. The librarian at the public library ad-

vises her to "get on base with hard work, make
second with courtesy, slide into third with a smile,
and come home with the winning run on pure grit. "

388   *Norton, Andre. Lavender-Green Magic. New York:
       Crowell, 1974. grades 4-9
When their father is listed as missing in action,
sixth-grader Holly and the twins, Judy and Crock,
find that their secure and comfortable world has
been shattered. When their mother finds a job, the
children must live with their paternal grandparents,
who are strangers to them. Besides living in a
different home without running water and electricity
and seeing their mother only on the weekends, the
children must learn to deal with living in a junkyard
and being almost the only blacks in a small school.
While helping her grandfather, Holly discovers an
herb pillow, which was used to help one sleep. When
Judy uses the pillow, she is led in a dream through
a maze. Waking up, Judy is able to lead Holly and
Crock through an overgrown garden to a house in
another century, where they become involved with
herbs and witches.

389   *Norton, Andre. Wraiths of Time. New York:
       Atheneum, 1976. grades 7+
An archaeology student, Tallahassee is employed
to catalog Sudan artifacts when she is asked to
identify a radioactive box. Opening the box reveals
an ankh (the ancient key to life that all Egyptian
gods and goddesses carried), which draws Tallahassee
through time and space into the ancient kingdom of
Meroe. In Meroe, she must pose as a Princess
Heir to save a civilization from takeover by evil
power-seekers. Tallahassee succeeds in her disguise, recovers the rod and ankh from the power-
seekers, escapes from being kidnapped, and makes
important decisions concerning strategy, but finds
that she cannot return to the present time.

390   **Smucker, Barbara. Runaway to Freedom: A Story
       of the Underground Railway. New York: Har-
       per & Row, 1977. grades 4-8
Twelve-year-old Julilly and Liza escape from a
Mississippi plantation with two other slaves. When
the two men are captured by slave-hunters, the two
girls continue to Canada and freedom on the Underground Railroad.

391   *Sterling, Dorothy. <u>Mary Jane.</u> Eau Claire, Wis.:
            Hale, 1968. grades 4-6
        Preparing to go into junior high, Mary Jane wants
        to go to Wilson High, a newly integrated junior and
        senior high school, rather than Douglass, where
        her older brother and sister went. One other black
        student will be starting seventh grade with her, but
        basketball practice takes a lot of his time, leaving
        Mary Jane by herself. It is her ability in science
        that finally helps her to become an accepted part
        of the school.

392   **Taylor, Mildred D. <u>Roll of Thunder, Hear My Cry</u>.
            New York: Dial, 1976. grades 7+
        Nine-year-old Cassie does not realize how lucky her
        family is to own land and not have to answer to
        anyone during the Depression. In 1933, Cassie
        begins to be aware of inequalities when their Mis-
        sissippi school gets the old, thrown-away books from
        the white school, they walk to school instead of
        having a bus, she is forced to apologize for bumping
        into a white girl, night riders burn and torment
        blacks, and Cassie's mother loses her teaching job.
        However, the Logan family is determined to main-
        tain their integrity, pride, and independence.

393   *Goble, Paul. The Girl Who Loved Wild Horses.
         Scarsdale, N. Y.: Bradbury, 1978. grades
         K-2
         An Indian girl loves wild horses and seems to have
         a special understanding of them. While she is with
         the horses, a thunderstorm scares them. In order
         not to be trampled, she grabs a horse's mane,
         rides with them, and remains with the herd.

394   *Udry, Janice May. The Sunflower Garden. Irving-
         ton, N. Y.: Harvey House, 1969. grades 2-
         5
         Pipsa, an Algonkian Indian, sees her father praise
         her older brothers, but she notices that he doesn't
         pay any attention to her. One day while Pipsa is
         weeding her sunflower garden, she hears a rattle-
         snake and finds it ready to bite her baby brother.
         She courageously kills the snake before it can strike
         and is satisfied when her father recognizes and
         praises her bravery.

395 *Anauta. <u>Wild Like the Foxes: The True Story of
        an Eskimo Girl</u>. New York: Day, 1956.
        grades 7-9
     Alea is a young Eskimo child. Her mother dies
     attempting to rescue the family's boat, which carries
     supplies for the next year. Not wanting to be sepa-
     rated, her father, brother, and Alea continue their
     life of trapping, hunting, and caring for themselves
     in their home in Labrador many miles from others.
     Alea becomes a good shot with a rifle, hunts and
     traps ceaselessly, and is full of the love of adven-
     ture. Although Alea is content with her life, her
     father feels that she is being deprived of female
     companionship and makes several attempts to alter
     that situation. When Alea insists that she is happy
     with her father and brother, further attempts are
     discontinued and she is allowed to remain with them.

396 *Beatty, Patricia. <u>Red Rock over the River</u>. New
        York: Morrow, 1973. grades 7-9
     Thirteen-year-old Dorcas Fox is the only girl at
     Fort Yuma in 1881 until fourteen-year-old Hattie
     Lou Mercer arrives guarding the Army wagon.
     Half-Indian, quite tall, and carrying a Winchester,
     Hattie Lou causes quite a stir in the fort. She
     becomes the housekeeper for the Fox household and
     makes life easier for Dorcas. Hattie Lou gives
     Dorcas courage to visit the Arizona Territorial
     Prison to help the inmates write letters and makes
     her aware of the horrible prison conditions. How-
     ever, Dorcas discovers that Hattie has her own
     reasons for visiting the prison, implementing a

prison escape, and finally disappearing.

397   **Butler, Beverly. A Girl Named Wendy. New York:
         Dodd, Mead, 1976. grades 8+
      Just two weeks away from her eighth-grade gradua-
      tion from the Indian mission school, Wendy receives
      a letter from her mother saying that she and her
      father aren't living together anymore. Her aunt
      and uncle want to take Wendy and her sister to live
      with them in Milwaukee, and their mother agrees.
      However, the two girls want to be with their mother
      and attempt to run away. They eventually go to
      live with their aunt and uncle, but the Indian and
      white ways conflict in Wendy as she strives to be
      her own person and decides to return to live with
      her mother.

398   **Capps, Benjamin. Woman Chief. Garden City,
         N.Y.: Doubleday, 1979. grades 9+
      Taken captive by the Crow when she is ten years
      old, Slave Girl, an Atsina Indian, must learn how
      she fits into Antelope Man's family. Wanting a
      young boy to replace his dead son, Antelope Man is
      very upset when he learns he has captured a young
      girl. However, Antelope Man discovers that Slave
      Girl prefers to be with him rather than with the
      women in the lodge. Slave Girl takes it upon her-
      self to tend the horses, gather twigs for arrow
      shafts, learn about the stars, shoot a bow and
      arrow, make arrowheads, hunt for game, and per-
      form many other duties generally given to males.
      When she becomes an adult, she becomes a chief.

399   *Embry, Margaret. Shadi. New York: Holiday
         House, 1971. grades 7+
      Shadi is the Navajo word for "my older sister."
      As the shadi, fourteen-year-old Emma assumes
      special responsibilities in the Cleveland family.
      When her father moves away, her mother has a
      baby, which Emma must help deliver. Her mother
      dies, and the baby is placed in an aunt's home.
      Taking the initiative, Emma runs away from school
      to get the baby and find another home for it. As
      tradition and the New Way conflict, Emma must
      select the best parts of each.

400   *George, Jean Craighead. Julie of the Wolves. New

York: Harper & Row, 1972. grades 7+
Running away from an unhappy past, thirteen-year-
old Julie becomes lost on the North Slope of Alaska
on her way to San Francisco to locate her father.
She becomes friends with and is accepted by a wolf
pack, which helps her to survive.

401   *Hamilton, Virginia. Arilla Sun Down. New York:
       Greenwillow, 1976. grades 7+
       Being part of an interracial family is difficult for
       twelve-year-old Arilla--she doesn't know where she
       belongs. Her mother is black, her father is part-
       black and part American Indian, and her older
       brother wants to be American Indian (Amerind, as
       he calls it). As a young child, Arilla lives as an
       Indian, but when her mother wants to return to her
       hometown to open a dance studio, Arilla has to
       change lifestyles and cultures. When Arilla saves
       her brother's life, she discovers her identity in the
       family.

402   *Hassler, Jon. Jemmy. New York: Atheneum,
       1980. grades 7+
       Jemmy is seventeen years old and a half-breed.
       Her mother, a Chippewa Indian, has been dead for
       six years, and her father is an unemployed alcoholic.
       When he tells Jemmy to quit school to have more
       time for housekeeping duties, she does it without
       questioning his motives. However, she spends her
       free time with the Chapmans, an artistic family.
       The Chapmans help to make a painter out of Jemmy
       and give her a different view of life. In her struggle
       to overcome poverty, Jemmy begins to understand
       her life, family, friendship, and nature.

403   **Johnson, Dorothy M. Buffalo Woman. New York:
       Dodd, Mead, 1977. grades 7+
       A member of the Oglala Indian tribe, Whirlwind's
       life from her birth in 1820 to her death in 1877 is
       related through customs, family and tribe relation-
       ships, and historical changes caused by the west-
       ward expansion of the United States. All the Buffalo
       Returning is the sequel.

404   **Knudson, R.R. Fox Running. New York: Avon,
       1975. grades 7+
       Returning from a track meet, nineteen-year-old

Kathy "Sudden" Hart, Champ, and Coach Calvin find
an Indian girl running across the desert oblivious to
loose sand, mesquite, and cactus. Amazed by her
speed and rhythm, they take her to Uinta University
with them, where Sudden is assigned to train and
take care of her. In this way, a deep and gentle
relationship develops between the two runners as
Fox Running overcomes her fear to become a com-
petitor in track events.

405   *Mulcahy, Lucille. Magic Fingers. New York:
           Nelson, 1958. grades 5-7
       Robert tells his family that he wants to attend the
       university in the fall. Having no income and a
       blind grandmother to care for, twelve-year-old
       Natachee wants her brother to get an education
       and bring honor to the pueblo. Natachee believes
       that her grandmother, who used to be the pueblo's
       best potter, can teach her to be a potter to earn
       money for Robert's tuition and their supplies.
       Natachee's persistence and confidence make their
       venture a success.

406   **O'Dell, Scott. Island of the Blue Dolphins. Boston:
           Houghton Mifflin, 1960. grades 7+
       In the early 1800s, as her tribe is leaving a de-
       serted island off the coast of California, twelve-
       year-old Karana spots her younger brother racing
       for the ship, but it is too late for them to turn
       back. Concerned for him, Karana jumps overboard
       to be with him. For eighteen years, Karana con-
       tends with a pack of wild dogs, which kill her brother;
       Aleutian sea-otter hunters; the environment; and lone-
       liness in order to survive. Zia is the sequel.

407   *Sobol, Rose. Woman Chief. New York: Dial,
           1976. grades 5-8
       Based on a true story, Woman Chief tells of Lone-
       some Star, who was born a Gros Ventre but was
       captured and raised as a Crow. Sharp Knife, into
       whose lodge she was placed, trained and encouraged
       her as a hunter and warrior. She attained the
       status of chief after achieving the four highest coups.

408   *Terris, Susan. Whirling Rainbows. Garden City,
           N.Y.: Doubleday, 1974. grades 6-9
       Being thirteen, adopted, Jewish, part-Indian, and

slightly overweight, Leah attends a summer camp
in Wisconsin hoping to discover her roots. Something about her personality (she is constantly talking
about her Indian heritage) and her cousin's teasing
set Leah up for the role of camp buffoon and all-
around scapegoat. Though the eight-week camp
seems very long at times, Leah wants to qualify
for the final canoe trip to the Ojibway Basin, where
she hopes to find an Indian relic. Although she
succeeds in qualifying for the canoe trip, Leah discovers that knowing who she is has nothing to do
with finding an Indian relic or learning about Indian
customs. She learns that being Indian is only part
of her total identity.

409   Coatsworth, Elizabeth. Marra's World. New York:
       Greenwillow, 1975. grades 2-6
       Marra is not pretty. She is clumsy, not very
       smart in school, and has no friends until Alison
       moves to the island. Alison discovers that Marra
       has much to offer--she is very aware of and knowl-
       edgeable about the island's environment. They learn
       from each other and gain mutual understanding.

410   Litchfield, Ada B. A Cane in Her Hand. Chicago:
       Whitman, 1977. grades 1-3
       Valerie is a visually impaired girl who learns ways
       to cope with her failing vision in a sighted world.

411   Naylor, Phyllis. Jennifer Jean, the Cross-Eyed
       Queen. Minneapolis: Lerner, 1967. grades
       K-5
       Although Jennifer Jean has crossed eyes and other
       children sometimes tease her, she doesn't really
       care because she can see her nose. When her
       parents tell her that she is going to a doctor to
       see if he can straighten her eyes, she wonders if
       she will be a different girl then. After she gets
       her glasses, she is not sure she likes them until
       a friend assures her that she is the same girl.

412 **Butler, Beverly. <u>Light a Single Candle</u>. New York:
Dodd, Mead, 1962. grades 7-9
Wanting to attend college and become an artist,
fourteen-year-old Cathy finds that she must change
her life after an operation for glaucoma leaves her
blind. She remains out of her regular school for
a semester while she begins to learn Braille, to
type, and to gain independence in a nonsighted world.
Because she fears being different or receiving
sympathy, Cathy decides to attend a school for the
blind, where she is constantly reminded that she is
blind and cannot succeed in a regular school. However, Cathy is determined to "light a single candle"
and succeed at as normal a life as she can, which
includes returning to her regular high school. The
sequel to this book is <u>Gift of Gold.</u>

413 **Cookson, Catherine. <u>Go Tell It to Mrs. Golightly.</u>
New York: Lothrop, Lee & Shepard, 1977.
grades 4+
When her father dies, eight-year-old Bella is sent
to live with her grandfather, her only relative. Although he prefers to live alone, Joseph Dodd reluctantly agrees to take Bella in for the holidays;
however, he is even more uneasy when he discovers
that she is blind. When her investigations lead
her and a friend into a kidnapping plot and they
are taken prisoner, Bella finds that her handicap is
advantageous in helping them escape. It is Bella's
disappearance as well as her lively personality that
help her grandfather to realize his loneliness and
his need for companionship.

414　**Corcoran, Barbara. <u>Axe Time/Sword Time</u>. New
　　　　York: Atheneum, 1976. grades 5-9
　　Elinor, who is seventeen years old, cannot read or
　　write well since she was hit by a golf ball when she
　　was younger. School has been difficult for her
　　since the accident, but her mother would like her
　　to go to college. Against her mother's wishes,
　　Elinor volunteers to be a plane spotter just before
　　the United States's involvement in World War II.
　　She later quits school to get an inspector job with
　　the Navy.

415　Corcoran, Barbara. <u>A Dance to Still Music.</u> New
　　　　York: Atheneum, 1974. grades 5-8
　　Fourteen-year-old Margaret has decided that "if
　　she couldn't be like other people, she'd just stay
　　by herself." Things have changed a lot for Mar-
　　garet since she lost her hearing because of an
　　illness--she loved music, but she can't enjoy it
　　anymore; her grandfather and aunts whom she loved
　　have died; and she and her mother have left Maine
　　to live in Florida. Now, her mother is going to
　　remarry, and Margaret doesn't want to be a burden
　　to her or attend a school for the handicapped. Mar-
　　garet runs away and finds friends--Josie and a deer--
　　who understand her, accept her, and give her self-
　　confidence. When Margaret writes to her mother
　　to tell of her plans to attend a workshop for the
　　deaf while living with Josie, her mother and hus-
　　band visit her and agree to let her try her plan.

416　*Curry, Jane Louise. <u>The Change Child.</u> New York:
　　　　Harcourt, Brace & World, 1969. grades 3-6
　　Because she has a lame leg, thirteen-year-old
　　Eilian is thought by the Welsh village people to be
　　a changeling, a fairy-child believed to have been
　　exchanged for a real child. Living during the reign
　　of Elizabeth I, Eilian knows she is different because
　　she enjoys composing poems and songs, likes sing-
　　ing, and wishes to play the harp. When it is feared
　　that Eilian may be stolen and forced to marry Ras-
　　tall, she is sent to her grandmother, who is be-
　　lieved to have magic powers. Her grandmother
　　attempts to marry Eilian to Rastall also, but Eilian
　　escapes to the kingdom of the Fair Folk, where she
　　discovers her true identity and ambition.

417   *Friis Baastad, Babbis. <u>Kristy's Courage</u>. New
       York: Harcourt, Brace & World, 1965.
       grades 4-6
       When Kristy is hit by a car, the doctors repair her
       cheek as well as they are able at the time; however,
       a dimple line and scar remain, and her mouth is
       twisted into a smile. Plastic surgery will be neces-
       sary later, but Kristy (a second-grader) must toler-
       ate classmates' staring and older boys' teasing at
       school. At home, she is lost in the confusion of
       an active younger brother and her mother's going
       to the hospital. However, Kristy finds a way to
       solve her own problem.

418   *Holland, Isabelle. <u>Dinah and the Green Fat King-</u>
       <u>dom.</u> Philadelphia: Lippincott, 1978. grades
       5-12
       Twelve-year-old Dinah has a weight problem, which
       her mother especially nags her about. In order to
       escape the nagging, Dinah retreats to Her Tree in
       a wood several blocks from her house. Here, she
       invents the Green Fat Kingdom, where the fattest
       people are the most beautiful and records her fan-
       tasies in a notebook. When she becomes angry with
       her family and runs away, Dinah discovers that she
       has been unfair to them. Through a discussion with
       her mother, Dinah is convinced that her mother
       loves her and decides to make an effort to accept
       herself.

419   **Hoover, H.M. <u>Children of Morrow</u>. New York:
       Four Winds, 1973. grades 5-9
       Living in a primitive militaristic society, twelve-
       year-old Tia and nine-year-old Rabbit are misfits.
       Slightly over five feet tall, Tia is as tall as an
       adult. Rabbit's unnatural quietness, squat body, and
       stammer make him the butt of cruel jokes and an
       outcast of his society. When Rabbit "mind-kills"
       an adult who is hurting Tia, the children must run
       away. Through telepathy, the children communicate
       with the people of Morrow, who arrange to meet
       them at The Sea. Although the trip is dangerous,
       Tia and Rabbit succeed in escaping and start a new
       life in Morrow.

420   **L'Engle, Madeleine. <u>The Young Unicorns.</u> New
       York: Farrar, Straus & Giroux, 1968. grades 7+

When ten-year-old Emily is accidentally blinded
during a robbery of two scientists' office, the
circumstances are thought to be peculiar; however,
it isn't until two years later that a serious investi-
gation is pursued. A budding musician, Emily continues to pursue her ambition of becoming a concert
pianist while Dave, an eighteen-year-old ex-gang
member, reads her lessons to her. When the
Austin children (Emily's friends) and Emily rub an
old lamp and a genie appears, a sense of impending
danger and suspense involves everyone as they seek
to solve the mystery.

421   *Little, Jean. From Anna. New York: Harper &
           Row, 1972. grades 4-6
       Nine-year-old Anna lives with her family in Germany
       in 1933. Her brothers and sisters do not include
       her in their games because she is so awkward.
       Her mother gets angry with her because she cannot
       seem to do anything right. Her father seems to
       understand and calls her a "special" child. After
       they move to Canada, a doctor discovers that Anna
       needs glasses and must attend a special school.
       At the school, Anna slowly and hesitantly makes
       friends and gains self-confidence as she makes a
       special gift and speaks perfect English to the family
       for the first time. Listen for the Singing is the
       sequel.

422   Little, Jean. Mine for Keeps. Boston: Little,
           Brown, 1962. grades 4-6
       It had always been Sal's wish to be able to live at
       home, but now that it has come true, she is afraid.
       Having cerebral palsy means that she has to walk
       with crutches, her hands get stiff (which makes
       buttons, zippers, and pencils difficult to use), she
       can't walk her dog, and she feels different. But,
       with her family's firm support and her dog, Sal
       finds that she can overcome some of her dependence,
       loneliness, and fear.

423   **McCaffrey, Anne. Dragonsong. New York:
           Atheneum, 1976. grades 5-9
       Having very traditional values and ideas, Menolly's
       father forbids her to compose songs, play instru-
       ments, teach music, and sing--all activities that
       she enjoys. When she cuts her hand, it appears

that her musical career is over. Unable to endure
a world without music, fifteen-year-old Menolly runs
away. When she happens upon a clutch of the planet's
fire-lizard eggs, she "impresses" nine of the hatch-
lings--an unprecedented feat--and is invited to take
music lessons from the Masterharper of Pern. The
sequels are Dragonsinger and Dragondrums.

424 **Mathis, Sharon Bell. Listen for the Fig Tree. New
       York: Viking, 1974. grades 7+
Although she is blind, sixteen-year-old Marvina
must have the strength to survive and help her
mother through this first Christmas since her father
was killed. Feeling lonely and bitter, Mrs. Johnson has begun drinking and blaming the police for
inaction--her husband was black. Marvina continues
to run the family (taking care of the checks, buying
groceries, cooking) even when her mother belittles
her and demands her rights. Without the hope of
Kwanza (a Black African harvest celebration) and
the help of Mr. Dale, Marvina would give up, but
she is determined to survive.

425 Murray, Michele. Nellie Cameron. New York:
       Seabury, 1971. grades 3-7
Nine-year-old Nellie is a middle child--not the
oldest and not the youngest. Reading has always
been difficult for her. Sometimes she hates words
and books and says she doesn't care if she can
read or not. Other times, she is determined to
show everyone (her family especially) that she is
not stupid and can learn to read. When she feels
that her reading clinic teacher cares about her,
Nellie becomes a different, more confident child
(at least in reading).

426 **Savitz, Harriet May. Run Don't Walk. New York:
       Watts, 1979. grades 9+
After a diving accident that leaves her unable to
walk, Samantha is returning after a year's absence
to graduate from high school. It is also Johnny's
senior year. Johnny, who has always been in a
wheelchair because of a curvature of the spine, has
just moved to town. Being a fighter, Johnny carries
on a personal demonstration against the school's
inadequate facilities for the handicapped. He tries
to get Sam involved. However, it isn't until her

goal of running in the marathon is shattered that
Sam realizes the frustrations that Johnny has been
experiencing. She must act.

427   *Yolen, Jane. <u>The Mermaid's Three Wisdoms.</u>
            Cleveland: Collins & World, 1978. grades 4+
A twelve-year-old hearing-impaired girl, Jess escapes from her hovering, over-concerned mother
and the rest of the hearing world by rowing her
dinghy out to sea and letting the motion calm her.
While she is on the sea, a mermaid (Melusina)
leaps from the water and disappears. Because she
has allowed herself to be seen, Melusina is banished
from her merfolk and forced to live on land. Jess
discovers that her hearing impairment helps her to
communicate with Melusina, since they must sign,
and the two girls become friends.

428   **De Angeli, Marguerite. <u>Thee, Hannah!</u> Garden
           City, N. Y.: Doubleday, 1940. grades 2-5
       Hannah, a nine-year-old Quaker girl, wishes she
       could wear pretty dresses and hats rather than her
       plain black clothes. However, when she befriends
       a runaway slave and her son, Hannah learns the
       meaning of the plain black hat.

429   **Turkle, Brinton. <u>Rachel and Obadiah.</u> New York:
           Dutton, 1978. grades K-3
       When a ship is sighted coming to Nantucket Island
       in the early 1800s, all the Quaker children want to
       be the one to spread the good news. The runner
       has always been a boy, but Rachel questions whether
       she might be picked as the runner when the next
       ship is sighted. To solve the question, a footrace
       is suggested between Rachel and her older brother
       Obadiah. With her persistence, Rachel wins the
       race, delivers the good news of a ship's arrival,
       and receives two coins before her brother arrives
       from his side trip to the berry patch.

---

430   *Blume, Judy.   Starring Sally J. Freedman As Her-
          self.   Scarsdale, N. Y.:   Bradbury, 1977.
          grades 4-7
       Sally, a ten-year-old Jewish girl, is growing up in
       New Jersey and Florida during and after World War
       II.   In order to avoid boredom, Sally creates ad-
       venture stories in which she stars--she is a famous
       detective who reveals Hitler's hiding place, a movie
       star, and an American volunteer who helps Jews to
       escape from Germany.

431   *Bodger, Joan.   Clever Lazy: The Girl Who In-
          vented Herself.   New York: Atheneum, 1979.
          all ages
       The baker and her husband make a trip to the shrine
       of the Goddess to ask for a baby girl who will be
       "clever enough to be lazy and lazy enough to be
       clever. "   Their wish is granted when Clever Lazy
       is born.   Allowed to explore, Clever Lazy discovers
       and invents many useful things.   She longs to be
       an inventor, and she receives her wish when she is
       asked to invent for the Emperor.   However, Clever
       Lazy faces a moral decision as she foresees the
       Emperor misusing his power.   She escapes from
       him, mysteriously disappears, and settles down to
       raise a family.

432   **Brenner, Barbara.   A Year in the Life of Rosie
          Bernard.   New York: Harper & Row, 1971.
          grades 3-7
       In Brooklyn in 1932, half-Jewish, ten-year-old Rosie
       learns about Hard Times--her mother's death, a

115

new stepmother, living with her grandparents, religious ambiguity, and the Depression. When Rosie discovers her similarity to her grandmother (their strong wills), she is more able to accept her grandmother's advice--"concentrate on the things you can change, and let the others go"--and finds that she can cope with life.

433   *Brown, Irene Bennett. Willow Whip. New York: Atheneum, 1979. grades 4-7
In Kansas in 1918, fourteen-year-old Willow wants her family to own a farm so they don't have to "be movers all their lives." She shoulders more than her share of the responsibility for the farm chores and crops, gathers and shells black walnuts, and traps in order to earn money for the down payment. In the process of gaining title to the farm, she denies herself fun and friendship and earns the nickname of "Willow the Whip" from her brothers and sisters. When she almost dies from sunstroke, Willow realizes what she has lost and promises herself to change--to bend in the wind.

434   *Colman, Hila. Chicano Girl. New York: Morrow, 1973. grades 7+
Donna, a sixteen-year-old Mexican-American, wants the wealth and material possessions of the American society, but she finds she cannot ignore her Mexican heritage. She decides that she must get involved in the cause for more acceptance and justice for her people.

435   *Colman, Hila. Rachel's Legacy. New York: Morrow, 1978. grades 6-9
Rachel, Ellie's mother, recalls her early childhood and womanhood as a poor Jewish immigrant. Her determination to avail herself and her family of everything America can provide makes her a business success. Ellie's Inheritance is the sequel.

436   **Cummings, Betty Sue. Now, Ameriky. New York: Atheneum, 1979. grades 7+
Because Brigid is nineteen and the eldest child, she is sailing to America in the 1840s to earn money. Since the potato famine in Ireland has made life difficult for her family, Brigid is to earn passage money for her brother to come to America. Then,

together, they are to work to reunite the family in America. Despite the hardships of adjusting to a new culture alone, Brigid succeeds in bringing her brother to America and finding the strength to be independent.

437   *Gates, Doris. Blue Willow. New York: Viking, 1940. grades 4-6
For ten-year-old Janey, the blue willow plate that was given to her by her mother means laughter, happiness, and a permanent home of their own. Since her father is a migrant worker in the San Joaquin Vally, Janey has not had friends, gone to a "regular" school, or had a real home in five years. When she gives up her willow plate to pay the rent, she wonders if she will ever see it again or have her dreams come true without it. Her courage allows her to say goodbye to the willow plate, but her courage also forces the truth to surface, and her permanent home is no longer a dream.

438   *Girion, Barbara. Like Everybody Else. New York: Scribner, 1980. grades 6-9
Twelve-year-old Sam (Samantha) thinks she has enough to worry about--junior high, her Bat Mitzvah, Lenny, and Jessica--without her mother writing a spicy adult novel. In having to deal with her embarrassment because of her mother's book and her decision not to run for a student-council position, Sam learns that "the important thing is find out what kind of a woman you are and not let anyone stop you." It is Sam's insight that helps her mother confront her book's rejection and her role.

439   **Greene, Bette. Summer of My German Soldier. New York: Dial, 1973. grades 7+
Twelve-year-old Patty Bergen lives in a small Southern town in the 1940s. During the summer, a group of German prisoners of war are brought to a POW camp outside Jenkinsville, Arkansas. When Anton, one of the POWs, escapes, Patty gives him food, shelter, and clothing. Being Jewish, Patty realizes their friendship is ironic, but Anton assures her that she is a person of value. Morning Is a Long Time Coming is the sequel.

440   **Jacob, Helen Pierce. The Diary of the Strawbridge

Place. New York: Atheneum, 1978. grades
3-7
Victory and Faith, thirteen-year-old twins, are
members of a Quaker family prior to the Civil
War. Because their farm is the last stop before
freedom in Canada for escaped slaves, the family
must be especially careful. The twins' quick thinking while a "shipment" is on the farm delays a
search party looking for five runaway slaves long
enough for the slaves to be transferred to the next
stop. This is the sequel to The Secret of the Strawbridge Place.

441   *Krasilovsky, Phyllis. LC is the Greatest. Nashville, Tenn.: Nelson, 1975. grades 6+
Thirteen-year-old Louise wants to show the world
that she is the greatest. Louise is Jewish, but
secretly wishes she were Christian like her girl-
friend. Growing up in Brooklyn during the Depression, Louise comes to terms with herself and
her parents--she is determined to try many things
and not be concerned about how she looks or what
others think of her.

442   *Madison, Winifred. Becky's Horse. New York:
Four Winds, 1975. grades 3-7
Becky, a seventh-grader, has always wished for a
horse, but she knows she can never have one: her
father is without work during the Depression. Her
father is also very concerned over a Jewish cousin
and his family back in Austria, which Hitler's
troops are invading. After trying to get a job at
a stable, Becky finds the way to get her dream
horse--by entering a contest. The agonizing decision Becky must make when she wins the horse
helps her know her purpose in life.

443   *Mays, Lucinda. The Other Shore. New York:
Atheneum, 1979. grades 5-10
Having waited for her father to send money for
their passage to America, Gabriella and her mother
struggle through five years in Italy with no word
from him or money for a year. When they finally
arrive in New York's Lower East Side in 1911,
Gabriella wishes to become "American" and attempts
to deny her Italian heritage. A tragic fire in a
sweatshop begins to bring Gabriella closer to her

family and her roots. While breaking the Italian
tradition against education for women by attending
high school and college, Gabriella also gains a new
respect and appreciation for her family.

444   Slobodkin, Florence and Louis. Sarah Somebody.
        New York: Vanguard, 1969. grades 7+
        Breaking with Jewish tradition, nine-year-old Sarah
        is allowed to go to school in Poland in 1893, al-
        though this may cause a hardship for the family.
        Sarah earns her identity because she is able to
        read and write.

445   *Smith, Nancy Covert. Josie's Handful of Quietness.
        Nashville, Tenn.: Abingdon, 1975. grades
        4-7
        Twelve-year-old Josie longs to have a permanent
        home, school, and friends and attend college to
        become a teacher. However, her family must
        follow the crops. During the summer in Ohio,
        while she is caring for her younger brother and
        sister as well as doing the housework, she becomes
        friends with Mr. Curtis. Mr. Curtis is an old
        man who is trying to keep his farm and orchard
        maintained so he won't have to sell them. Josie
        discovers the solution to both her problem and Mr.
        Curtis's--hire her father to manage Mr. Curtis's
        farm.

446   **Snedeker, Caroline Dale. Downright Dencey.
        Garden City, N.Y.: Doubleday, 1927. grades
        3-7
        Living in the early 1800s on Nantucket Island,
        Dionis Coffyn, a young Quaker girl, throws a
        stone that hits Sam Jetsam. Knowing violence is
        against her religion, Dencey feels doubly responsible
        and asks Sam for forgiveness. However, Sam will
        not forgive her unless she teaches him to read.
        Dencey teaches Sam (despite his bad reputation)
        until her mother discovers that she has been meet-
        ing him. When Dencey refuses to promise to stay
        away from Sam, she is punished. But when Sam
        saves Dencey's life he is welcomed into the Coffyn
        family, where he learns about education, religion,
        family relationships, and love.

447   *Sorensen, Virginia. Plain Girl. New York: Har-

court, Brace & World, 1955. grades 4-6
Being Amish, ten-year-old Esther wears plain dark
clothes without buttons and does not attend public
school. However, school officials come to tell her
father that Esther must attend school or he will be
jailed. Old memories of Daniel, Esther's older
brother, are renewed. Her father believes that
school started Daniel thinking about new and different
ways, which encouraged him to run away. Esther
meets a friend at school. However, it is this
feeling of friendship and talking with Daniel that
help Esther to discover that she has to decide some
things for herself and help her accept the good parts
of the new world and of the old tradition.

448 **Weiman, Eiveen. Which Way Courage. New
York: Atheneum, 1981. grades 4-7
Living in modern-day Pennsylvania, fourteen-year-
old Courage belongs to the Old Order Amish, who
do not accept modern conveniences. Although education is generally allowed only through the eighth
grade, Courage receives permission from her re-
luctant father to continue for one year at the high
school so she can help care for Jason, her younger
brother, who has spina bifida. After Jason dies
and with many reservations about marriage, her
plain life, and the Amish custom of unquestioning
obedience, Courage decides to leave her family
to live in the city with an uncle and his family.

449   **Gauch, Patricia Lee. <u>This Time, Tempe Wick?</u>
      New York: Coward, McCann & Geoghegan,
      1974. grades 2-6
      Tempe Wick is a "most surprising girl" who lives
      during the Revolutionary War. She is surprising
      in that she races her horse, wrestles, and works
      at the plow better than anyone else. However, in
      the winter of 1781, the unhappy, starving, and un-
      paid Pennsylvanian soldiers mutiny and turn against
      the people who have helped and fed them. When
      two soldiers attempt to take Tempe's horse, she
      becomes angry and more determined to keep her
      property. With courage and quick thinking, Tempe
      boards her horse in the house, stands guard over
      her property for three days, and finally physically
      pushes the soldiers out the door.

450   **Goldreich, Gloria and Esther. <u>What Can She Be?</u>
      series. New York: Lothrop, Lee & Shepard,
      1972-81. grades 1-5
      This series features women in many nontraditional
      professions--architect, computer scientist, farmer,
      film producer, geologist, lawyer, legislator, mu-
      sician, newscaster, police officer, scientist, and
      veterinarian. Relevant information, including vo-
      cabulary, is provided for each job.

451   Harler, Anne. <u>Sports Stars--Tracy Austin: Teen-
      age Champion.</u> Chicago: Childrens Press,
      1980. grades 2-6
      The youngest woman ever to win the Women's
      Singles U.S. Open at Forest Hill, New York

sixteen-year-old Tracy Austin has played tennis
since she was three. Her concentration, speed, and
strength have earned her respect from her opponents.
Tracy's goal is to be ranked Number 1 in the world.

452   *Johnston, Johanna. Harriet and the Runaway Book:
       The Story of Harriet Beecher Stowe and Uncle
       Tom's Cabin. New York: Harper & Row,
       1977. grades 2-6
As a child, Harriet was energetic, quick to learn,
and clever, but she was not a boy. All that was
expected of girls was that they become a wife and
mother or a teacher. Harriet felt that she was a
slave just as much as the blacks. Having seen and
heard many situations in which slaves were mis-
treated, Harriet wanted to be able to help free them.
In writing Uncle Tom's Cabin, she felt as if she
had helped expose the evils of slavery and gain
some freedom.

453   *Latham, Jean Lee. Elizabeth Blackwell: Pioneer
       Woman Doctor. Champaign, Ill.: Garrard,
       1975. grades 2-5
Coming from a family where it was believed that
girls were thinking creatures and deserved the same
education as boys, Elizabeth Blackwell had to face
loneliness, hardship, and prejudice in order to become a doctor. While encouraging her sister and
other women in becoming doctors, Elizabeth also
opened her own hospital in New York as well as
the first medical college in England.

454   *McGovern, Ann. Shark Lady: True Adventures of
       Eugenie Clark. New York: Four Winds, 1978.
       grades 1-5
Since she was nine years old, Eugenie Clark has
been fascinated by fish, especially sharks. She
set up her own aquarium at home. In college,
she studied to become an ichthyologist. After
graduation, Eugenie researched sharks around the
world, becoming the director of a marine labora-
tory and a professor of zoology.

455   Morse, A.R. Tennis Champion: Billie Jean King.
       Mankato, Minn.: Creative Educational Society,
       1976. grades 2-6
Through her tennis playing, Billie Jean has shown

that women are serious athletic competitors. Having won more tennis championships than anyone else, Billie Jean also helps other women in their sports careers.

456 *Parlin, John. Amelia Earhart. New York: Dell, 1974. grades 2-5
Even as a girl, Amelia looked for excitement. When airplanes were invented, Amelia was very interested and vowed that one day she would become a pilot. She worked hard at many jobs and eventually was the first woman to fly across the Atlantic.

457   *Aldis, Dorothy. Nothing Is Impossible: The Story
         of Beatrix Potter. New York: Atheneum,
         1969. grades 3-7
      As a child, Beatrix seldom sees her parents. They
      live in one part of the house while Beatrix lives in
      another. Except for her nurse, Beatrix talks with
      few people. Her grandmother starts her thinking
      about a future when she insists that the family
      should do something with their lives and not just
      exist. As an adult, Beatrix Potter's career of
      picture-book author and illustrator is initiated when
      she is asked to write to a sick child.

458   **Banner, Lois W. Elizabeth Cady Stanton: A Radi-
         cal for Woman's Rights. Boston: Little,
         Brown, 1980. grades 7+
      Raised in a conservative family and influenced by
      the liberal family of her cousin, Elizabeth is faced
      with attempting to reconcile the two opposing ele-
      ments. Her mother emphasizes the domestic arts,
      duty, submission, and order. However, learning
      from her father's law office that women are unfairly
      treated, Elizabeth carries the crusade for women's
      rights throughout New England.

459   *Barton, Peter. Staying Power: Performing Artists
         Talk About Their Lives. New York: Dial,
         1980. grades 7+
      Interviews with twelve performing artists (half of
      them female) are presented. Musicians, dancers,
      and actors recount the decisions, sacrifices, pres-
      sures, and recognition of being a performing artist.

It is their determination to grow that gives them
staying power.

460 *Booth, Arthur H. The True Story of Queen Victoria. Chicago: Childrens Press, 1964.
grades 5+
Having the longest reign in British history, Queen
Victoria enjoyed power. Extremely reserved, Victoria was known for her firmness, cool detachment,
and self-reliance. The Victorian period was an
age of exploration and invention--railroads, auto-
mobiles, telephones, phonographs, cameras, moving
pictures, and electricity.

461 Canary, Martha. Life & Adventures of Calamity
Jane. Wheatland, Wyo.: Triple R, 1970.
grades 5+
In rescuing the wounded Army Post commander during an Indian raid, Martha Cannary was called "Calamity Jane." Her adventurous life included jobs
as a teamster, nurse, Pony Express rider, hunter,
rancher, wife, and mother.

462 Caudill, Rebecca. Florence Nightingale. Evans-
ton, Ill.: Row, Peterson, 1953. grades 4-6
Not interested in becoming a fashionable young lady,
Florence becomes one of the most highly educated
women of her day. Supported only by her father,
Flo is determined to get nursing training. During
the Crimean War, Florence, recognizing the need
for sanitary conditions, nutrition, and professional
nurses, founds modern nursing.

463 *Clairmonte, Glenn. Calamity Was the Name for
Jane. Denver: Sage, 1959. grades 9+
A frontierswoman, Calamity Jane was one of the
most independent people who ever lived. She showed
great courage and performed many kind deeds.

464 *DeClue, Denise. Women Shaping History. Milwaukee: Raintree, 1979. grades 4-8
This book presents brief biographies of women
prominent in the women's movements: Anne Hutchinson, Lucretia Mott, Elizabeth Cady Stanton, So-
journer Truth, Lucy Stone, Betty Friedan, and
Gloria Steinem.

465   de Grummond, Lena Young, and Delaune, Lynn de
        Grummond. <u>Babe Didrikson: Girl Athlete.</u>
        Indianapolis: Bobbs-Merrill, 1963. grades
        3-7
        Always in a hurry, Babe races from one activity
        to another but always doing the best she can. As
        a youngster, she plays baseball and marbles with
        the boys. As she grows up, she practices any
        sport until she has each detail mastered. It's not
        a wonder that she becomes the greatest woman
        athlete of the century.

466   de Leeuw, Adele. <u>Marie Curie: Woman of Genius.</u>
        Champaign, Ill.: Garrard, 1970. grades 5+
        Determined to get an education and know everything
        about everything, Marie (called Manya by her family)
        works as a tutor and governess to put her older
        sister through school so she in turn can help finance
        Manya's education. Finally, she is able to attend
        the university in Paris to study physics. Here,
        she meets Pierre Curie, whom she marries. To-
        gether, they set up a laboratory. Their discovery
        of radium earns them the Nobel Prize.

467   *Dolan, Edward F., Jr., and Lyttle, Richard B.
        <u>Janet Guthrie: First Woman Driver at</u>
        <u>Indianapolis.</u> Garden City, N.Y.: Doubleday,
        1978. grades 4-9
        Having a love of adventure, Janet enjoys flying and
        parachuting, tries to enter a program to train women
        astronauts, and becomes a sports-car racing driver.
        These are her interests before she is asked to be
        a championship-car racing driver. Whatever happens
        at Indy, Janet will try her best.

468   Dunham, Montrew. <u>Anne Bradstreet: Young Puritan</u>
        <u>Poet.</u> Indianapolis: Bobbs-Merrill, 1969.
        grades 3-7
        As a child, Anne Bradstreet enjoys reading and
        exploring. Her love for reading prompts her father
        to hire a tutor to teach her Latin, Greek, and
        French, since girls are not allowed to attend schools.
        It is after Anne moves to America as an adult that
        she begins writing poetry. Published in England,
        her collection of poems, <u>The Tenth Muse,</u> is the
        first book written by an American woman.

469   *Epstein, Sam and Beryl. <u>She Never Looked Back:</u>
            <u>Margaret Mead in Samoa.</u> New York: Coward,
            McCann & Geoghegan, 1980. grades 3-7
        Believing in her father's statement that "adding to
        the world's store of knowledge is the most important
        thing a human being can do," Margaret becomes an
        anthropologist doing fieldwork in the South Pacific.
        After her first book, <u>Coming of Age in Samoa,</u>
        Margaret's reputation as a scientist is acknowledged.
        She states, contrary to the popular belief of the
        day, that behavior is learned, not inborn.

470   Faber, Doris. <u>Colony Leader: Anne Hutchinson.</u>
            Champaign, Ill.: Garrard, 1970. grades 4+
        For defending her freedom of conscience in the
        Massachusetts Bay Colony, Anne Hutchinson is ban-
        ished from the Puritan church and the colony and
        is forced to settle in Rhode Island and Long Island.
        Wanting to continue her father's work as a minister,
        Anne is able to find a way, notwithstanding many
        frustrations and trials.

471   *Faber, Doris. <u>Oh, Lizzie! The Life of Elizabeth</u>
            <u>Cady Stanton.</u> New York: Lothrop, Lee &
            Shepard, 1972. grades 5+
        Even when she was young, Lizzie "could always be
        counted on to do the unexpected." Lizzie discovers
        early that boys are preferred and men have legal
        advantages. Because of this, she endeavors to
        gain equal rights for women throughout her life by
        helping to organize the Seneca Falls Convention
        and draft the Declaration of Rights and Sentiments.

472   *Facklam, Margery. <u>Wild Animals, Gentle Women.</u>
            New York: Harcourt Brace Jovanovich, 1978.
            grades 7+
        Dealing with ethology, or the study of animals in
        their own habitat, the book relates the experiences
        of eleven women scientists who have studied animals
        in the air, on the land, and in the sea. The
        animals range from owls to giant pandas to sharks.

473   *Fisher, Aileen. <u>Jeanne d'Arc.</u> New York:
            Crowell, 1970. grades 3-5
        At fifteen, Jeanne d'Arc hears the voice of St.
        Michael telling her that she must save the French

city of Orleans from the English; that she must ensure that the Dauphin, the heir to the French throne, is crowned King Charles VII; and that she must drive the English out of France. She leads the French people into battle against the English, but is burned at the stake for her efforts.

474   Foote, Patricia. Girls Can Be Anything They Want.
        New York: Messner, 1980. grades 4-8
The book contains biographies of fifteen women currently involved in careers previously considered "for men only"--surgeon, politician, lawyer, psychiatrist, aerospace engineer, gynecologist, harness-racing driver, airline pilot, fire fighter, medical social worker, television producer, astronaut trainee, dentist, karate instructor, and trucking terminal manager.

475   **Fox, Mary Virginia. Lady for the Defense: A
        Biography of Belva Lockwood. New York:
        Harcourt Brace Jovanovich, 1975. grades 9+
Believing that "there's almost nothing a girl can't do as well as a boy when she's given the chance," Belva overcomes tragedy and disappointment to prove her point. She becomes the first woman lawyer in the United States and the first female presidential candidate.

476   *French, Laura, and Stewart, Diana. Women in
        Business. Milwaukee: Raintree, 1979.
        grades 4-8
Short biographies of notable businesswomen: Mercedes Bates, Coco Chanel, Jane Evans, Barbara Gardner Proctor, Dorothy Shaver, and Irma Wyman.

477   *Harmelink, Barbara. Florence Nightingale: Founder
        of Modern Nursing. New York: Watts, 1969.
        grades 7+
Florence is the troublemaker in the Nightingale family because she feels compelled to oppose her parents' wishes. Driven by her conviction that God has "called" her to serve Him, Flo finally breaks away from her family to become a nurse. Through the years, Flo becomes proud, cold, and ruthlessly ambitious. She sacrifices everything to her work, even her health and family, since she considers her work in nursing to be of utmost importance.

478   Jacobs, William Jay. <u>Mother, Aunt Susan and Me.</u>
       New York: Coward, McCann & Geoghegan,
       1979. grades 4-6
       At sixteen, Harriot Stanton describes her mother,
       Elizabeth Cady Stanton, and a close friend, Susan
       B. Anthony, in their fight for women's equal rights
       in the mid-1800s. Harriot tells how her free-
       thinking family helped her to be active in the suffrage
       movement.

479   **James, Naomi. <u>Alone Around the World.</u> New
       York: Coward, McCann & Geoghegan, 1979.
       grades 9+
       As a child, Naomi was shy and adventurous. As
       she grew older, she found that she still liked being
       alone. She liked to travel and discovered that she
       wanted to have control of her own future--to be
       able to choose, not just accept. Finally, after try-
       ing several activities, Naomi fantasizes her goal
       of singlehandedly sailing nonstop around the world
       (the first time for a woman). Naomi, having only
       two years' sailing experience, accomplishes her goal
       and also breaks the record for speed.

480   *Kendall, Alan. <u>Elizabeth I.</u> New York: St. Mar-
       tin, 1975. grades 9+
       Perhaps the most famous monarch in English history,
       Queen Elizabeth I's reign is a golden age. Her
       aptitude for learning makes her one of the most
       talented princesses of the sixteenth century. Deal-
       ing with Catholicism and Protestantism, Parliament,
       foreign invasion, marriage, and her cousin Mary
       Queen of Scots, Elizabeth I has to walk a thin line,
       which she effectively accomplishes.

481   *Laklan, Carli. <u>Golden Girls: True Stories of
       Olympic Women Stars.</u> New York: McGraw-
       Hill, 1980. grades 7-10
       More than twenty sportswomen from the early
       twentieth century to the more recent years are
       discussed along with a short history of the Olympic
       games. The problems, training, skill, and disci-
       pline necessary to become an Olympic gold medalist
       show these women for the champions they are.

482   *Leone, Bruno. <u>Maria Montessori: Knight of the
       Child.</u> St. Paul, Minn.: Greenhaven, 1978.
       grades 5-8

Although her family wants her to become a teacher,
Maria decides that she will be a medical doctor.
She is the first woman medical student and becomes
the first woman doctor in Italy. When she becomes
interested in educating children, Dr.
Montessori
develops new materials that stress self-learning and
organizes a system for training teachers (named for
its originator).

483 *McFerran, Ann. Elizabeth Blackwell: First Woman
Doctor. New York: Grosset & Dunlap, 1966.
grades 5+
A radical for his day, Elizabeth's father believes
and impresses upon his daughters that all humans
are equal and that girls should be as well educated
as boys. Elizabeth, a very determined child, feels
that being a doctor is a different thing to do, a
way to challenge herself. She becomes the first
female doctor.

484 *McLenighan, Valjean. Women and Science. Mil-
waukee: Raintree, 1979. grades 4-8
Brief biographies of women in science: Annie Jump
Cannon, astronomer; Rachel Carson, biologist; Alice
Hamilton, doctor; Margaret Mead, anthropologist;
Florence Sabin, medical researcher; and Chien
Shiung Wu, physicist.

485 *McLenighan, Valjean. Women Who Dared. Mil-
waukee: Raintree, 1979. grades 4-8
Biographies of adventurous women: Margaret
Bourke-White, photographer; Mrs. E. J. Guerin,
mountaineer; Janet Guthrie, race-car driver; Diana
Nyad, swimmer; Kitty O'Neil, stuntwoman; and
Annie Smith Peck, mountaineer.

486 *McReynolds, Ginny. Women in Power. Milwaukee:
Raintree, 1979. grades 4-8
Brief descriptions of the lives of women in politics:
Ella Grasso, Elizabeth Holtzman, Barbara Jordan,
Juanita Kreps, Golda Meir, and Jeannette Rankin.

487 *Madison, Arnold. Carry Nation. Nashville, Tenn.:
Nelson, 1977. grades 9+
When Carry is a child, "she is inclined to be a
tomboy, is very strong willed and absolutely afraid
of nothing." She has a dominating personality and

always insists on having her own way. From these
early beginnings, Carry proceeds to carry her fight
for temperance from one saloon to another, smash-
ing their stores of liquor.

488   **Merriam, Eve. Independent Voices. New York:
Atheneum, 1968. grades 5+
These seven heroes and heroines were chosen
"because they seemed to be not heroic." They lived
according to what was best for themselves and others.
Biographies of three women are presented in verse--
Elizabeth Blackwell, Lucretia Mott, and Ida B.
Wells.

489   **Morgan, Helen L. Maria Mitchell: First Lady of
American Astronomy. Philadelphia: West-
minster, 1977. grades 7-10
From her father, who is an amateur astronomer,
Maria learns about the stars. When her brother
leaves home to become a sailor, Maria is upset
because she is not allowed to go; however, she
becomes her father's assistant for recording whatever happens in the sky. Always stubborn, Maria
questions and wants proof of everything. When she
discovers a comet, Maria begins an amazing career,
which includes delving into areas previously denied
women.

490   *Morrison, Dorothy Nafus. Ladies Were Not Expected: Abigail Scott Duniway and Women's
Rights. New York: Atheneum, 1977. grades
4-7
Life was traditional for Abigail until her husband
had an accident. When she had to support the
family, she loved it! She went from school-teaching
to running a shop to editing one of the first news-
papers in Portland. Resenting the injustices to
women, she began her fight for women's suffrage
in Oregon.

491   *Nathan, Dorothy. Women of Courage. New York:
Random House, 1964. grades 5-9
Profiles of Susan B. Anthony, Jane Addams, Mary
McLeod Bethune, Amelia Earhart, and Margaret
Mead are presented.

492   *Opfell, Olga S. The Lady Laureates: Women Who

Have Won the Nobel Prize. Metuchen, N. J.:
Scarecrow, 1978. grades 9+
From Marie Curie in 1903 to Rosalyn Yalow in
1977, the personal and professional lives of the
seventeen women who have won the Nobel Prizes in
peace, literature, and science are described.

493 **Rice, Edward. Margaret Mead: A Portrait. New
York: Harper & Row, 1979. grades 7+
America's best-known anthropologist, Margaret said
that it was her active, decisive, loving, and intelligent grandmother who had the most influence on her
life. Her first trip to Samoa becomes one of
anthropology's best examples of fieldwork and the
subject of a best-selling book, Coming of Age in
Samoa.

494 *Riedman, Sarah R. Men and Women Behind the
Atom. London: Abelard-Schuman, 1958.
grades 7+
Marie Curie and her daughter, Irene Joliot-Curie,
represent the women in these biographical sketches
of people responsible for the discovery of atomic
energy.

495 **Ross, Pat, comp. Young and Female. New York:
Random House, 1972. grades 6+
Turning points in the lives of eight women are
described: Shirley MacLaine, Shirley Chisholm,
Dorothy Day, Emily Hahn, Margaret Sanger, Althea
Gibson, Edna Ferber, and Margaret Bourke-White.

496 **Sharpe, Mitchell R. "It Is I, Sea Gull": Valentina
Tereshkova, First Woman in Space. New
York: Crowell, 1975. grades 7+
On June 16, 1963, Valentina Tereshkova, Russia's
first woman cosmonaut, became the first woman
in space. Since childhood, she had done daring
things. In her teens, she was a parachutist.
Valentina's courage, independence, and intelligence
combined to make her an extraordinary person.
Today, she is a graduate aerospace engineer.

497 **Siegel, Beatrice. An Eye On the World: Margaret
Bourke-White, Photographer. New York:
Warne, 1980. grades 5+
Even as a ten-year-old, Margaret is determined to

do "all things that women never do." Through her
photography, Margaret shows the horrors of poverty,
famine, and war. Even when Parkinson's disease
begins to make her job difficult, her energy, inge-
nuity, and perseverance refuse to let her quit working.

498   *Smith, Senator Margaret Chase, and Jeffers, H.
       Paul. Gallant Women. New York: McGraw-
       Hill, 1968. grades 5+
Short descriptions of the climactic events in the
lives of Anne Hutchinson, Dolly Madison, Harriet
Tubman, Harriet Beecher Stowe, Clara Barton,
Elizabeth Blackwell, Susan B. Anthony, Annie Sullivan, Amelia Earhart, Althea Gibson, Frances Perkins, and Eleanor Roosevelt.

499   **Sochen, June. Herstory: A Women's View of
       American History. New York: Alfred, 1974.
       grades 9+
This "feminist-humanist" commentary on American
history includes coverage of minorities (blacks,
children, and American Indians) who also lived in
America's past. It shows the consistency of white
Anglo-Saxon male attitudes and behavior toward all
human beings other than themselves. The book contains forgotten material about the other half of the
human beings who have lived in the United States.

500   **Sterling, Philip. Sea and Earth: The Life of Rachel
       Carson. New York: Crowell, 1970. grades
       5-8
Brought up with an appreciation of nature, Rachel
continues her interest in ecology throughout her life.
This interest forms the basis for her book Silent
Spring, which alerts everyone to the dangers of
pesticides and other chemicals that pollute the en-
vironment.

501   *Terry, Walter. Frontiers of Dance: The Life of
       Martha Graham. New York: Crowell, 1975.
       grades 5-9
When Martha Graham looks back over her life, she
remembers her father's observation--"You always
reveal yourself to me through movement"--as being
her very first dancing lesson. Martha applied this
insight as a dancer, choreographer, and teacher and

is considered a pioneer of modern dance.

502   *Tomkins, Mary E. <u>Ida M. Tarbell.</u> New York:
      Twayne, 1974. grades 9+
      As a muckraker, Ida Minerva Tarbell writes <u>History
      of the Standard Oil Company</u> in 1904, which signals
      a stop to unregulated monopoly in the oil industry.

503   *Washburn, Robert Collyer. <u>The Life and Times of
      Lydia E. Pinkham.</u> New York: Putnam, 1931.
      grades 9+
      A landmark in the emancipation of women is Lydia's
      founding of her Vegetable Compound business. Due
      to unstable family economic conditions, she markets
      her home remedy of herbs and alcohol, which gains
      its reputation through word of mouth as going "to
      the root of all female complaints." Lydia is "a
      pioneer of women's interest in woman, or woman's
      tacit antagonism to man."

504   *Wayne, Bennett, ed. <u>Women Who Dared to Be
      Different.</u> Champaign, Ill.: Garrard, 1973.
      grades 5-12
      The stories of four unusual women are told: Nellie
      Bly, reporter; Annie Oakley, sharpshooter; Maria
      Mitchell, astronomer; and Amelia Earhart, pilot.

505   *Werstein, Irving. <u>Labor's Defiant Lady: The
      Story of Mother Jones.</u> New York: Crowell,
      1969. grades 5-8
      One of the most militant trade-union organizers in
      the American labor movement, Mary Harris Jones
      is no ordinary woman. Wherever labor trouble
      breaks out, Mother Jones is there. She is labor's
      Joan of Arc--"the patron saint of picket lines." In
      attempting to abolish child labor, Mother Jones leads
      marches of mill children, which, however, are not
      successful.

506   **The Western Writers of America. <u>The Women Who
      Made the West.</u> Garden City, N.Y.: Double-
      day, 1980. grades 9+
      The lives of eighteen women who helped to settle
      the West are depicted. These lesser-known women
      were nurses, teachers, reformers, horse-traders,
      businesswomen, ranchers, peddlers, doctors, or
      newspaperwomen.

507 *Williams, Neville. The Life and Times of Elizabeth
I. Garden City, N.Y.: Doubleday, 1972.
grades 9+
"The first monarch to give her name to an age,"
Queen Elizabeth leads the English people to attain
a true national consciousness. Being "born mere
English," Elizabeth intends to rule with as much
authority as her father had and feels that being
Queen of England is her entire vocation.

508 *Yolen, Jane H. Pirates in Petticoats. New York:
McKay, 1963. grades 7-9
Although most pirates were men, several names of
women pirates are recorded--Fanny Campbell, Lady
Killigrew, Madame Ching, Lai Choi San, Anne Bonney, Mary Read, and others. Their stories make
interesting and exciting reading.

509 **Zochert, Donald. Laura: The Life of Laura Ingalls Wilder. Chicago: Regnery, 1976.
grades 9+
The biography of the author of the Little House
books is presented, including the years not covered
in the series. Laura's real life gives evidence for
her books--which makes them even more alive.

BLACK
NONFICTION, PRIMARY

---

510   **Lawrence, Jacob. Harriet and the Promised Land.
       New York: Simon & Schuster, 1968. grades
       Preschool-3
       This picture book shows Harriet Tubman's life as
       a slave and as the leader of groups of slaves to
       freedom.

511   *Brownmiller, Susan.   Shirley Chisholm: A Biogra-
            phy. Garden City, N.Y.: Doubleday, 1970.
        grades 5-8
        As a child living in Barbados with her grandmother,
        Shirley is a conscientious and eager student. After
        she comes to New York City with her family, she
        continues to be a good student. Three women in
        history especially influence Shirley: Harriet Tubman,
        Susan B. Anthony, and Mary McLeod Bethune. It
        isn't until her senior year in college that a professor
        suggests that she would do well in politics. As the
        first black woman to be elected to Congress, Shirley
        becomes a national figure overnight.

512   **Gaines, Ernest J.   The Autobiography of Miss Jane
            Pittman. New York: Dial, 1971. grades 9+
        A fictional biography, this book was written after
        nine months of interviews with Miss Jane, her
        family, and friends. Although the material was
        edited, it seeks to retain the language and style of
        Miss Jane. Born in slavery in Louisiana, Miss
        Jane Pittman lived to see the second emancipation
        a hundred years later.

513   **Graham, Shirley.   The Story of Phillis Wheatley.
            New York: Messner, 1949. grades 7+
        Brought as a young child from her African home-
        land to Boston, Phillis is bought by Mrs. Wheatley
        in 1761, although she is not intended to be a slave.
        Given a superior education, Phillis reads the poets,
        knows the classics, translates from Latin, and
        writes poetry. It is her pre-Revolutionary War

verse that establishes her reputation as a poet and
remains a testament to her passion for freedom.

514   Greenfield, Eloise. <u>Mary McLeod Bethune.</u> New
           York: Crowell, 1977. grades 3-5
In a family of sixteen, Mary thinks about going to
school and being able to read. However, there are
no schools for blacks until Mary is eleven. After
getting married, Mary decides to start a school
for black children, which she calls the Daytona
Normal and Industrial School for Girls. Later,
she also establishes a hospital for blacks.

515   Griffin, Judith Berry. <u>Phoebe and the General.</u>
           New York: Coward, McCann & Geoghegan,
           1977. grades 3-6
During the Revolutionary War, some people, thinking
that the American colonies should be ruled by the
king, feel that this might be accomplished by killing
General George Washington. Sam Fraunces, a
freed slave, had heard of such a plot. When Washington is to visit New York City, Sam asks his
thirteen-year-old daughter, Phoebe, to act as a spy
to discover the plot. She succeeds in her mission
and saves General Washington.

516   *Haskins, James. <u>Barbara Jordan.</u> New York:
           Dial, 1977. grades 7+
During her sophomore year in high school, Barbara
knows that she wants to become a lawyer. Despite
the fact that she is a black woman, Barbara is
determined to be "something outstanding"--she becomes
the first black woman Texas state senator and the
first to represent a southern state in the House of
Representatives.

517   **Haskins, James. <u>I'm Gonna Make You Love Me:</u>
           <u>The Story of Diana Ross.</u> New York: Dial,
           1980. grades 6+
The second of six children, Diana vies for attention
from her parents and the white and black communi-
ties. Her parents raise the family "to learn to take
care of themselves and ... to learn to be the best
at whatever they tried to do." Brought up with
music, Diana excels at singing and is determined
to be somebody. Her musical and acting abilities
eventually earn her the success she desires.

518 **Heidish, Marcy. A Woman Called Moses. Boston:
     Houghton Mifflin, 1976. grades 9+
     The story is based on the life of Harriet Tubman
     from her youth, when she sees her sister in a
     "coffle" gang, and through her adulthood as she
     conducts slaves on the Underground Railroad.

519 *Morse, Charles and Ann. Roberta Flack. Mankato,
     Minn.: Creative Education, 1975. grades 3-6
     Roberta says that she is just like the songs she
     sings--"loving, gullible, supersensitive, extremely
     emotional." The book tells of Roberta's childhood,
     her challenges, and her rise as a star pop musi-
     cian.

520 **Noble, Jeanne. Beautiful, Also, Are the Souls of
     My Black Sisters: A History of the Black
     Woman in America. Englewood Cliffs, N.J.:
     Prentice-Hall, 1978. grades 9+
     This book penetrates the myths and stereotypes
     surrounding America's black women to show the
     special problems they have faced and the contribu-
     tions they have made. It details the lives and works
     of leading black women, past and present.

521 Patterson, Lillie. Coretta Scott King. Champaign,
     Ill.: Garrard, 1977. grades 3-6
     Since childhood, Coretta has known the importance
     of education in the black struggle for equal rights.
     Her strong will has seen her through frustration,
     disappointment, and tragedy as she has worked to
     carry on her husband's ventures for peace and
     human rights.

---

522 **Brown, Marion Marsh. <u>Homeward the Arrow's</u>
<u>Flight</u>. Nashville, Tenn.: Abingdon, 1980.
grades 7+
Proud of the La Flesche name (which means "the
arrow"), Susan searches for a way to serve the
Omaha people. Believing in education, her father
sends his daughters away to school so they will fit
into society. Susan's familiarity with medical
tragedies that could have been prevented motivates
her to choose a career in medicine. With persistence and hard work, Susan La Flesche becomes
the first American Indian woman to become a doctor.

523 *Buehrle, Marie Cecilia. <u>Kateri of the Mohawks</u>.
Milwaukee: Bruce, 1954. grades 7+
With her face scarred from smallpox and her eye-
sight severely impaired, Kateri is left an orphan
to be cared for by her aunt and uncle. In her short
life, Kateri is converted to Christianity and vows
to be celibate at a time when tradition dictates that
a young woman marry.

524 Bulla, Clyde Robert. <u>Pocahontas and the Strangers.</u>
New York: Crowell, 1971. grades 5-8
As a young child, Pocahontas is curious about the
white men who come to her land in America. Since
no one is really able to answer her questions satis-
factorily, Pocahontas and her brother set out to
discover the answers themselves. Unafraid of the
white men, Pocahontas tries to understand her
father's cautious and distrusting attitude and attempts
to bring peace, but she is betrayed by her own people.

525 *de Leeuw, Adele. Maria Tallchief: American
Ballerina. Champaign, Ill.: Garrard, 1971.
grades 4-7
Her mother wishes her to become a pianist, although
Betty Marie secretly prefers dancing. Even as a
young child, Betty Marie and her sister Marjorie
carry full practice schedules for both piano and
dancing. After strenuous practice sessions with
the best teachers, Betty Marie is given her chance
to appear as a prima ballerina.

526 Felton, Harold W. Nancy Ward, Cherokee. New
York: Dodd, Mead, 1975. grades 4-6
Her Indian name was Nanye'hi, but her English
name was Nancy Ward. Following her husband into
battle against the Creeks, Nancy took up his wagon
against the enemy when he was killed, and her
courage helped her people to win the battle. For
her deed, Nancy was made Ghigau, a "Beloved
Woman" of the nation, who could sit in the highest
councils of the Cherokee nation. Since that time,
Nancy attempted to be the peacemaker between her
people and the Americans and English.

527 *Foreman, Carolyn Thomas. Indian Women Chiefs.
Washington, D.C.: Zenger, 1976. grades 8+
Different tribal traditions regarding female chiefs
and accounts of women rulers are described.

528 *Hartley, Lucie. Pauline Johnson: The Story of an
American Indian. Minneapolis: Dillon, 1978.
grades 5+
The life of Pauline Johnson, "a famous Canadian
poet and a fiery spokeswoman for Native Americans,"
is told. A Mohawk, Pauline lived during the nineteenth century and became known as a great en-
tertainer through her poetry-reading performances.

529 **Katz, Jane B. I Am the Fire of Time: The Voices
of Native American Women. New York:
Dutton, 1977. grades 9+
An anthology of the writings of past and present
Native American women, this book contradicts the
popular stereotype of the native woman as a "beast
of burden." The literature shows that in the total
culture, there was a harmonious blending of male
and female roles.

530 **Morrison, Dorothy Nafus. <u>Chief Sarah: Sarah</u>
<u>Winnemucca's Fight for Indian Rights.</u> New
York: Atheneum, 1980. grades 5-9
Called the Indian Joan of Arc, Sarah Winnemucca
fought to gain and protect the rights of the Indian
people. As scout, lecturer, author, educator, and
lobbyist, Sarah attempted to promote understanding
of her people's problems.

531 *Nelson, Mary Carroll. <u>Annie Waunkea: The Story</u>
<u>of an American Indian.</u> Minneapolis: Dillon,
1972. grades 5+
Annie was the first woman ever elected to the Navajo
Tribal Council, worked to improve the health and
welfare of the Navajo people, and was awarded the
Medal of Freedom in 1963.

532 *Niethammer, Carolyn. <u>Daughters of the Earth:</u>
<u>The Lives and Legends of American Indian</u>
<u>Women.</u> New York: Macmillan, 1977. grades
9+
Stressing the Native American woman's point of
view, the book describes various tribes' customs
and women's lives from birth to death. Although
the white female pioneer's life was similar in many
ways, the Indian woman generally enjoyed a good
deal more independence and security. Indian women's
roles, both traditional and nontraditional, are depicted.

533 *Seymour, Flora Warren. <u>Women of Trail and Wig-</u>
<u>wam.</u> New York: Women's Press, 1930.
grades 9+
Playing an important part in United States history,
several Native American women are featured in this
book of earlier history.

534 *Skold, Betty Westrom. <u>Sacagawea: The Story of</u>
<u>an American Indian.</u> Minneapolis: Dillon,
1978. grades 5+
As a young Shoshone child, Sacagawea is captured
by a group of raiding Hidatsa warriors. Made to
work in the fields with the women, Sacagawea serves
her master. Later, she is traded to a French-
Canadian fur-trader, Toussaint Charbonneau, for a
gambling debt, and becomes his wife. When he is
engaged as an interpreter, he, Sacagawea, and their

young son, Pompy, accompany the Lewis and Clark
Expedition, in which Sacagawea proves to be in-
valuable.

535   Waltrip, Lela and Rufus. <u>Indian Women: Thirteen</u>
       <u>Who Played a Part in the History of America</u>
       <u>from Earliest Days to Now.</u> New York: Mc-
       Kay, 1964. grades 9+
Until recent times, several American Indian tribes
gave women a higher position in their way of life
than women enjoyed among white societies. This
book tells of the lives of thirteen Native American
women who have contributed to American history.

---

536 **Hocken, Sheila. <u>Emma & I.</u> New York: Dutton, 1978. grades 8+
Growing up "seeing" things and people differently, Sheila does not know that she is different. She confronts all obstacles in an effort to be as independent as possible. When it seems that she will have to depend on others, Emma, her seeing-eye dog, leads her through many dangers. Finally, after twenty-eight years of darkness, Sheila has an operation that gives her normal vision.

537 **Frank, Anne. <u>The Diary of a Young Girl.</u> New
         York: Pocket Books, 1975. grades 9+
     During the Nazi occupation of Holland, eight people
     hide in the upper back portion of an office building
     in order to escape persecution for being Jewish.
     Their daily relationships, thoughts, and fears are
     expressed through thirteen-year-old Anne's diary
     entries.

538 **Morris, Terry. <u>Shalom, Golda.</u> New York:
         Hawthorn, 1971. grades 7-9
     A practical idealist, Golda is always ready to
     translate her idealism into action. When she is ten
     years old in Milwaukee, Golda organizes the Ameri-
     can Young Sister Society to collect money to buy
     textbooks for the needy. As an adult in Palestine,
     Golda joins the Haganah, the defense force, when
     the Jewish community is threatened. Later, she
     enters the Israeli government to become Prime
     Minister. "Only those who dare, who have the
     courage to dream, can really accomplish something, "
     Golda believes.

539 Robison, Nancy. <u>Nancy Lopez: Wonder Woman of</u>
         <u>Golf.</u> Chicago: Childrens Press, 1979.
         grades 3-5
     When Nancy began playing golf at age eight, she
     didn't know that by the time she was sixteen she
     would be the top-ranked amateur golfer in the world,
     or at twenty-three, she would be named the LPGA
     Rookie and Player of the Year. Nancy attributes
     her success to concentration and practice.

540   *Willcoxen, Harriett.   First Lady of India: The
               Story of Indira Gandhi.   Garden City, N. Y.:
               Doubleday, 1969.   grades 7-9
       Wanting to take a more active part in the drive for
       India's independence, Indu forms the Monkey Brigade,
       which gathers information and delivers messages
       among the Congress Party leaders.   Always active
       and interested in politics, Indira is elected president
       of the Indian National Congress, head of the Minis-
       try of Information and Broadcasting, and Prime
       Minister.

APPENDIX: CHRONOLOGY OF NOTABLE WOMEN

The * before the date indicates that at least one book is contained in the bibliography concerning that person or event.

c. 2300 B. C. --Tausert, an Egyptian queen, was the first woman to rule as pharaoh.

c. 1503-1482 B. C. --Queen Hatshepsut, who took the full title and regalia of a pharaoh, has been called "the first great woman in history" by the noted Egyptologist James Breasted.

c. 1200 B. C. --Bands of women called Amazons lived near the Thermodon River in the Black Sea region.

c. 1125 B. C. --Deborah, a judge, prophetess, and heroine of the Old Testament, inspired and led the Israelites to a great victory over their Canaanite oppressors.

c. 950 B. C. --The Queen of Sheba, a biblical character, journeyed as her own ambassador to King Solomon in her search for knowledge and truth.

c. 900 B. C. --Sammuramat, an Assyrian queen, led troops into battle.

c. 800 B. C. --Princess Elissa (or Dido), a Phoenician, left Tyre to found her own city, Carthage.

c. 700 B. C. --The "Laws of Gortyna," concerning inheritance, land tenure, marriage, and adoption, and dealing to a large extent with women's rights, were discovered in 1906 in Crete.

c. 500 B. C. --The Greek Perictione wrote Wisdom and the

Harmony of Women. Diotima was a priestess of Mantinea and a teacher of Socrates. Sappho was a poet and head of a girls' school.

c. 484-481 B. C. --Carian queen Artemisia led both a land and a naval army under Xerxes in the battle of Salamis of the Greco-Persian War.

*c. 400 B. C. --Women were excluded as spectators and participants during the Golden Age of the Greek Olympic Games. Women then instituted their own version of the Olympics, known as the Heraea; however, only foot races were held.

69-30 B. C. --Cleopatra was the queen of Egypt.

27 B. C. --Livia Drusilla, wife of Augustus and mother of Tiberius, is referred to as the "Founder of the Roman Empire."

23 B. C. --Amanirenas, Queen of Meroe, led the Ethiopian army that attacked the Roman army in Egypt to recover a portion of their land. The Ethiopians were defeated.

62 A. D. --Boadicea, queen of the Iceni (a tribe in eastern Britain), led her people in a revolt against their Roman overlords.

c. 100--Gerardesca Manutius of Syracuse was a gladiator star of the Roman Colosseum for eleven months, during which time she killed 200 people.

c. 300--Helena, concubine mother of Emperor Constantine, was the first woman to play a direct role in the support of Christianity.

385-415--Hypatia, a Roman, was a brilliant mathematician and philosopher.

c. 500--Pulcheria was an active stateswoman, playing an important part in resolving East-West and Church-State conflicts. As a scholar, she was trained in medicine and natural science, but she also taught her brother, Emperor Theodosius II, horsemanship and military strategy.

526--Empress Theodora, wife of Justinian, ruled the Byzantine

Empire as an equal and independent colleague with her husband.

c. 545(50)-613--Brunhild, a Visigothic princess, continued the fight to avenge her sister's death and aspired to the rule of Austrasia and Burgundy.

625-705--Wu Hou was the only empress in Chinese history.

c. 700--Huneberc, an Anglo-Saxon nun of Heidenheim, wrote the Hodoeporicon of St. Willibald, the only narrative extant of the pilgrimage to the Holy Land in the eighth century.

753-803--Byzantine Empress Irene the Athenian was the first woman in recorded European history to reign as a sovereign monarch.

c. 855--"Pope Joan" is reputed to have held the papal office; however, there is no truth in the story of the woman pope.

c. 1000--Trotula wrote Diseases of Women and Their Cure and coauthored an encyclopedia of medicine.

978?-1031?--Lady Murasaki of Japan wrote The Tale of Genji, considered the world's first novel.

1083--Anna Comnena founded and taught in a medical school in Constantinople.

1097-1291--During the Crusades, women participated in jousting tournaments dressed as their husbands.

1098-1178--St. Hildegarde, abbess of St. Rupert at Bingen, was the most prolific writer of the Middle Ages.

c. 1100--In Byzantium, Anna Comnena wrote Alexiad, an eyewitness account of the First Crusade.

1122-1202--Eleanor of Aquitaine accompanied her first husband, Louis VII, on the Crusade of 1147 and ruled her kingdom of Aquitaine in France. Eleanor also advanced the medieval institution of Courtly Love.

1200s--The Guglielmites believed that women were the only hope for the salvation of mankind. They proclaimed

that a female incarnation of the Holy Spirit, Guglielma
of Milan, was to establish a new church ruled by a
female pope and female cardinals.

1320s--The Jewish Sarah St. Giles conducted a large private
medical school for women at Montpellier.

c. 1373-c. 1440--Margery Kempe, a mystic, was the author of
the first extant autobiography in English.

1389-1429--Christine de Pisan was an Italian-born poet, novelist, historian, and writer on contemporary national and
international affairs.

*1412-1431--Joan of Arc was the most famous woman warrior
of the Middle Ages.

1498--Juliana Bremers, a British nun, wrote Treatyse of
Fysshynge wyth an Angle, which was one of the first
how-to books on the sport.

1532(35)-1625--Sofonisba Anguisila was the first Italian woman
to become an international celebrity as an artist and
the first for whom a substantial body of works is
known.

1554--A 3,000-woman army fought in three regiments while
defending Vienna.

*1558-1603--Queen Elizabeth I, whose name is given to a
period of history, was one of the greatest of all English rulers.

*1591-1643--Anne Hutchinson, of colonial America, was a
general practitioner and a founder of Rhode Island
(1638).

*1607--Pocahontas (1595-1617), a colonial Indian figure, inter-
ceded to save Captain John Smith, military leader of
the Jamestown settlement.

1616--Artemisia Gentileschi (1590-c. 1642) was the first woman
to join the Accademia del Disegno, a painters' guild,
and to have a major influence on the painting of her
day.

1640s--Quakerism extended equal opportunities to its women
since its beginning.

1642--Margaret Brent (1600?-1671?) was the first woman
lawyer in the colonies and probably the first feminist.
In 1648, she became the first woman in the world's
history to demand the right of suffrage.

*1650--Anne Bradstreet (1612?-1672), in accord with advanced
modern ideas, wrote poetry in which she expressed
her opposition to man's domination. She is considered
the first woman writer of significance from the colonies.

1701--Elizabeth Haddon (1680-1762) was one of the few women
to found a town--Haddonfield, New Jersey.

1716--Mary Butterworth (1686-1775) led a highly successful
counterfeiting ring in Plymouth Colony, Massachusetts,
by copying Rhode Island's pound "bills of credit."

1728-1814--Mercy Otis Warren was the most important woman
intellectual of the Revolution.

1755-1842--Marie Louise Elisabeth Vigee-Lebrun was the
court painter to Marie Antoinette.

*1773--Phillis Wheatley (1753?-1784), a slave who was brought
from Africa to Boston in 1761, wrote a volume of
Poems on Various Subjects, Religious and Moral,
which was published in London.

1775--Mary Katherine Goddard (1738-1816), the first post-
mistress of the United States, also printed the Decla-
ration of Independence.

1777--Sybil Ludington (1761-1839), at 16, rode 40 miles to
spread the word that the British were attacking the
region's munition stores.

*1782--Deborah Sampson (1760-1827), disguised as a man
named Robert Shirtliffe, served in the army during
the Revolutionary War.

1792--Mary Wollstonecraft Godwin (1759-1797), British, was
the first person to discuss woman's place in society
in explicitly political terms in her Vindication of the
Rights of Woman.

1794--Susanna Haswell Rowson (1762?-1824) wrote Charlotte

Temple, the first American bestseller, which went through more than 200 editions.

1795-1852--Frances Wright, speaking on liberalized divorce laws, birth control, free education run by the state, and the political organization of the working classes, was one of the first women orators.

*1797?-1883--Sojourner Truth, a former slave and domestic worker, was an evangelist active in both the abolitionist and women's movements. Appointed counselor to the freedmen by President Lincoln, she worked with the Freedmen's Bureau on behalf of former slaves.

1802-1887--Dorothea Dix was a crusader for prison and mental institution reform.

*1804--Sacajawea (1786?-1812), a Shoshone Indian woman, went with the Lewis and Clark expedition as a guide and interpreter.

1810-1850--Margaret Fuller published her pioneering and classic feminist work Women in the Nineteenth Century in 1845, was the leading American literary critic of the time, and became the first American woman to work as a foreign correspondent (for the New York Tribune in 1846).

1813--Dr. James Miranda Barry (1797-1865), who successfully impersonated a man for over 50 years, became Britain's first woman doctor.

1818-1894--Amelia Jenks Bloomer began a newspaper for women (the Lily) in 1849--probably the first to be edited entirely by a woman--and wore the "Turkish trousers" that were named for her.

1819-1910--Julia Ward Howe wrote "Battle Hymn of the Republic," which became the semiofficial Civil War song of the Union army, and was the first woman elected to the American Academy of Arts and Letters.

*1820-1906--Susan B. Anthony, called the Napoleon of the women's-rights movement, forged a national organization for the movement.

1821--Emma Hart Willard (1787-1870), determined to provide

women with a "male" education, founded the Troy Female Seminary, a school to train women as teachers.

*1823-1913--Harriet Tubman, after escaping from slavery herself, was called the Moses of her people when she returned to the South several times to lead other slaves to freedom. In 1862, she also served as a spy and scout for the Union in South Carolina.

*1830-1930--Mary Harris Jones, called "Mother Jones," devoted her life to organizing workers in all industries and helped found the Industrial Workers of the World (1905).

1831-1892--Amelia Ann Blanford Edwards, with R. Stuart Poole in 1882, started the Egypt Exploration Fund, which supports archaeological expeditions to excavate sites and publish records of the digs.

1834--Oberlin was the first college in the United States to admit women and blacks.

1837--Sarah Hale (1788-1879) edited Godey's Lady's Book, one of the first magazines to accept advertising, and made it into the most influential and widely circulated women's magazine published in the country up to that time.

*1837-1901--Queen Victoria, who had the longest reign in English history, is remembered for the dignity and respect she restored to the crown.

1838-1927--Victoria Woodhull, a member of the avant-garde fringe of the American reform movement, spoke for socialism, an end to the nation state, a single moral standard for men and women, and free love.

1838-1914--Margaret E. Knight, called a "woman Edison," was one of the most prolific women inventors (27 patents) and was unusual in her interest in heavy machinery.

1839--Constance Talbot, of England, was the world's first woman photographer.

1844-1923--Sarah Bernhardt was called the greatest actress of the French theater.

1844-1926--Mary Stevenson Cassatt painted in the Impressionist style with an interest in experiment and in using bright colors inspired by the out-of-doors.

*1844-1891--Sarah Winnemucca, a Piute, played the role of peacemaker in clashes between her people and the whites and wrote Life Among the Piutes, "the first outbreak of the American Indian in human literature."

1845--Laura Haviland (1808-1898) was known as the "President of the Underground" for her work in helping escaped slaves.

*1847--Maria Mitchell (1818-1889), an astronomer, discovered a comet, which bears her name.

1848--The Seneca Falls Convention, which marked the beginning of the women's-rights movement, was called by Elizabeth Cady Stanton (1815-1902), the most effective feminist of her day, and Lucretia Mott (1793-1880).

1848-1889--Belle Starr, nicknamed the "bandit queen," was a well-known woman outlaw.

*1849--Elizabeth Blackwell (1821-1910) became the first accredited woman doctor in the United States.

1850--Elizabeth Smith Miller (1822-1911) designed and wore the first trouser outfit for women.

*1852--Harriet Beecher Stowe (1811-1896) wrote Uncle Tom's Cabin, which exerted an influence equaled by few other novels in history, helped solidify both pro- and anti-slavery sentiment, and fanned the flames of the Civil War.

*1852-1903--Calamity Jane, a famous character of the West, was said to be able to "out-drink, out-cuss, and out-fight" any man.

1853--Pauline Wright Davis (1813-1876) was the founder of the first feminist newspaper, The Una. She also helped organize and presided at the first National Woman's Rights Convention in Worcester in 1850.

1853--Antoinette L. Brown (1825-1921) became the first woman minister in the United States when she was ordained in the Congregational Church.

*1854--Florence Nightingale (1820-1910) was the founder of modern nursing, raising it from a menial job to a respected profession.

1855--The marriage of Lucy Stone (1818-1893) and Henry Blackwell provided a model for reform: she maintained her maiden name and career, and the partnership was an equal and permanent one.

1855--The University of Iowa became the first state university to admit women on an equal basis with men.

1855--Laura Keene (1820?-1873) was the first woman in the United States to be a major theatrical producer.

1857--Nettie Fowler McCormick (1835-1923), an astute businesswoman, helped to consolidate her husband's farm-machine industry into what would become the International Harvester Company.

1859-1947--Carrie Chapman Catt was the Superintendent of Schools in Mason City, Iowa (the first woman to hold such a high administrative position in the public-school system), founded the Women's Peace Party in collaboration with Jane Addams, called for the establishment of a League of Women Voters, and led the woman-suffrage campaign (second only to Susan B. Anthony).

1860-1935--Charlotte Perkins Gilman, who wrote Women and Economics, was the most influential feminist thinker of the early twentieth century.

1861--Vassar, the first women's college to offer a liberal-arts education, was founded after Lydia Booth, Matthew Vassar's niece, encouraged him to establish a college for women.

1863-1930--Mary Whiton Calkins became the first woman elected president of the American Psychological Association (1905), was accorded a similar honor by the American Philosophical Association (1918), and was the first American woman to attain distinction in either field.

1864-1952--Frances B. Johnston, a celebrated documentary photographer in the years leading up to World War I, became known as "the photographer of the American court" from taking pictures of life in the White House.

1865--Dr. Mary Walker (1832-1919), the only woman ever to receive the Medal of Honor, was given the award for her services in the Union Army as a medical officer.

1866--Dr. Lucy B. Hobbs (1833-1910) was the first American woman to obtain a Doctor of Dentistry degree.

1867-1919--Sarah Breedlove Walker, known as Madame C. J. Walker, made a fortune manufacturing hair-straightener lotions and skin preparations for blacks and founded the largest black-owned business in the nation (1910).

1868--Revolution, the first important women's-rights paper to appear after abolition, was established by Susan B. Anthony and Elizabeth Cady Stanton.

1869--The Wyoming territory gave its female citizens the right to vote, making them the only legally enfranchised women in the world. Esther Morris (1814-1902), who was largely responsible for the victory, became Wyoming's first woman justice of the peace.

1869-1940--Emma Goldman, believing that woman's emancipation depended upon sexual liberation, urged women to break loose from the traditional ideas that restricted their ability to experience all life had to offer--to reclaim their sexuality--through the use of birth-control methods.

1869--Arabella "Belle" Mansfield (1846-1911), from Iowa, became the first woman to be admitted to the bar in the United States; however, she never practiced law.

*1869--Susan B. Anthony became chairwoman of the executive committee of the National Woman Suffrage Association. In 1892, she was elected its first president.

1870--Susan Smith McKinney Steward (1847-1918) became the first black woman to receive the M.D. degree.

1871--George Eliot (Marian or Mary Ann Evans) (1819-1880), called the most distinguished English woman novelist,

wrote Middlemarch, considered by Tolstoy to be the
finest novel in the English language.

1872--Victoria Claflin Woodhull, from New York, was the
presidential nominee of her National Radical Reform
party--the first woman nominated for the presidency.

1872--Charlotte Ray (1850-1911) was the first black woman
lawyer to practice in the United States.

1872--Susan B. Anthony, attempting to vote under the terms
of the Fourteenth Amendment, was arrested, tried,
and sentenced.

1873-1949--May Wilson Preston was the first woman member
of the Society of Illustrators.

1873--Ellen H. Swallow Richards (1842-1911) was the first
woman to graduate from the Massachusetts Institute
of Technology. In 1879, she was elected as the first
woman member of the American Institute of Mining
and Metallurgical Engineers.

1873--The Supreme Court used "rational basis" ("Man is, or
should be, woman's protector and defender. The natural and proper timidity and delicacy which belongs
to the female sex evidently unfits it for many of the
occupations of civil life.") to uphold a sexually dis-
criminatory law. "Rational basis" was used to uphold
laws through the 1960s.

*1873--Belva Lockwood (1830-1917), one of the most effective
advocates of women's rights of her time, became the
first practicing woman lawyer in the United States when
she was admitted to the District of Columbia bar. In
1879, she became the first woman to be admitted to practice before the Supreme Court.

1874--Louise Blanchard Bethune (1856-1913) was the first professional American woman architect. In 1888, she
became the first woman elected to membership in the
American Institute of Architects.

1876--Sarah Ann Hackett Stevenson (1841-1909) became the
American Medical Association's first woman member.

1876--Anna Bissell, enterprising wife of the inventor of the

Bissell carpet sweeper, nurtured the company to financial maturity.

*1876--Lydia Pinkham (1819-1883) marketed a highly profitable home remedy concocted of roots, seeds, and alcohol to cure ills ranging from sterility to kidney distress. By 1898, the compound was the most widely advertised product in the United States.

1878--Emma M. Nutt was America's first female telephone operator.

1879--Mary Mahoney (1845-1926) became the first black professional nurse in the United States.

1879--Mary Baker Eddy (1821-1910) founded the Church of Christ, Scientist.

1880-1928--Emma B. Freeman was a photographer of the early West.

1880-1966--Helen Keller, blind and deaf, and her teacher, Anne Sullivan Macy (1866-1936), were pioneers for the handicapped.

*1881--Clara Barton (1821-1912), "Angel of the Battlefield" during the Civil War, founded the American Red Cross.

1882-1941--Virginia Woolf, English novelist, critic, and essayist, was one of the first explorers of the feminine consciousness. Her work greatly influenced the art of the modern novel.

*1883-1966--Margaret Higgins Sanger organized the American birth-control movement in the early twentieth century and helped found the International Planned Parenthood Federation.

*1884--Belva Lockwood, nominated by the Equal Rights Party, was the first woman to run formally for the office of President of the United States.

*1884-1962--Eleanor Roosevelt, probably the world's most admired woman in her time, was a noted humanitarian, author, UN delegate, and active force in the Democratic Party.

*1885--Elizabeth Cochrane Seaman (1867-1922), better known

as "Nellie Bly," was the first famous woman reporter in the United States. She is known for her solo completion of an around-the-world trip in fewer than eighty days.

1887- --Georgia O'Keeffe is generally recognized as one of the most original and productive of American painters.

*1889--Susan La Flesche (1854-1903) was the first American Indian woman to become a doctor.

1890--Josephine Shaw Lowell (1843-1905) and Maud Nathan (1862-1946) founded the New York Consumers League with the purpose of improving shop and factory conditions under which women and girls had to work.

1891--Ruth Cleveland (1891-1904), daughter of President Grover Cleveland, had the Baby Ruth candy bar named after her.

1891--Fannie Barrier Williams (1855-1944) founded the first nursing school for black women at Provident Hospital in Chicago.

1891--Ida Bell Wells-Barnett (1862-1931) was a pioneer black woman activist and journalist. In 1910, she founded and became first president of the Negro Fellowship League.

1892--Frances Ellen Watkins Harper (1825-1911) wrote Iola Leroy; or Shadows Uplifted, the first novel published by a black American woman. She also helped found the National Association of Colored Women.

1892--Clelia Duel Mosher, researcher and physician, conducted the earliest known systematic study of the sexual habits and attitudes of American women.

1893--Queen Isabella (1451-1504) was the first queen and the first noncitizen to appear on a United States stamp.

1893--The Women's Building, considered one of the most important exhibits of the Chicago World's Fair Columbian Exposition, was coordinated, designed, and decorated entirely by women. Mrs. Potter Palmer, president of the Board of Lady Managers, was instrumental in its success. Sophia G. Hayden of Boston was the architect. Alice Rideout, San Francisco, and Enid Yandell, Louisville, were the ornamentation designers.

1893-1967--Dorothy Parker, an author renowned for her rapier wit, came to epitomize the liberated woman of the twenties.

*1894-   --Martha Graham, a major figure in modern dance, was the first choreographer to combine pure dance ideas with psychological comment. Her choreographic career is one of the longest and most fertile of any artist in history.

*1894-1906--Ida Minerva Tarbell (1857-1944), the first woman muckraker in the United States, exposed political and industrial corruption. Her work culminated in a two-volume book, The History of the Standard Oil Company.

1895-   --Anna Freud, daughter of Sigmund Freud, was considered the most outstanding living psychoanalyst by her colleagues.

1895-1965--Dorothea Lange was praised by Edward Steichen as the "greatest documentary photographer" in the United States during the Depression.

1896--Mary Church Terrell (1863-1954) helped organize, and became the first president of, the National Association of Colored Women.

*1896--Since the first year of the modern Olympics, the ironclad rule stating that no woman shall be allowed to compete, with men or with each other, in a contact sport still remains. A woman named Melpomene was refused entry in an ancient Greek Olympic marathon race.

1899--Alice Guy-Blache (1873-1965), the first woman film director in the world, directed the first narrative film.

*by 1900--The territories of Wyoming, Utah, Colorado, and Idaho had granted women the right to vote. (It is interesting to note that where farming and farm women were of critical importance, the women first won recognition of their equality.)

1900--Women were admitted to the Olympic Games in tennis

singles, mixed doubles, and golf. Caroline Cooper of
Great Britain won the tennis singles and was the first
woman to win at a modern Olympic Games. Margaret
Abbot, winner of the golf competition, was the first
American woman to win an Olympic event.

1902- --Leni Riefenstahl, German actress and director, is
best known for her direction of Triumph of the Will
(1934), the record of the Nazi Rally at Nuremberg
which remains a masterpiece of lyrical propaganda;
and Olympiad (1936-1938), the film record of the 1936
Olympic Games, which remains the finest record of
the Olympics yet made.

1902--Martha Washington (1731-1802) became the first white
American woman to appear on a United States postage
stamp.

*1902--Beatrix Potter (1866-1943) illustrated her own book,
The Tale of Peter Rabbit, which is considered the
first "modern picture book."

1903--Margaret Dreir Robins (1868-1945) was one of several
people who organized the Woman's Trade Union League
in an effort to help working women organize unions.

*1903--The Polish woman Marie Curie (1867-1934), the first
woman ever to be awarded the Nobel Prize, was also
the first person ever to receive two Nobel awards--
one for the discovery of radioactivity, the other for
the isolation of pure radium (1911).

1903--Emmeline Pankhurst (1858-1928) with her daughters,
Christabel (1880-1958) and Sylvia (1882-1960), founded
Britain's Women's Social and Political Union (WSPU),
which developed into a radical organization using mil-
itant tactics to lobby for suffrage.

1904--Bertha Pappenheim (1859-1936), born in Vienna, founded
the Jewish feminist movement in Germany by encouraging Jewish women to demand political, economic, and
social rights and by organizing a nationwide network
of Jewish social workers whose concern was the protection and emancipation of women.

1905--Lucia Parsons, a Chicana, was one of the leaders and
founders of the International Workers of the World, a

labor organization, and fought for the rights of workers, protection of the poor, and liberation of women.

*1907--Pocahontas was the first Indian to appear on a United States postage stamp.

1908--Beatrice Moses Hinkle (1874-1953), with Dr. Charles R. Dana, established the first American psychotherapeutic clinic, at Cornell Medical College.

*1909--Selma Lagerlof (1858-1940), from Sweden, was the first woman to receive the Nobel Prize in Literature.

1909--Isadora Duncan (1878-1927) revolted against traditional dance form by replacing the traditional tutu with loose, long, flowing, often transparent garments and emphasizing emotion.

1908, 1910--Helena Rubenstein (1871-1965) and Elizabeth Arden (1884-1966) each founded a cosmetics corporation which elevated the use of beauty aids to an acceptable part of all women's lives.

c. 1910-1960--Katharine Cornell (1893-1974), Lynn Fontanne (1887?-), and Helen Hayes (1900-) shared claim to the rank of first lady of the American theater.

1910-1981--Mary Lou Williams, jazz pianist and arranger, is considered to be the first successful woman jazz instrumentalist.

1911-1972--Mahalia Jackson was known as the "Gospel Queen."

1912--Juliette Gordon Low (1860-1927) founded the Girl Scouts of America.

1912--Women were allowed to compete for the first time in the swimming events of the Olympics.

*1914--Gabrielle "Coco" Chanel (1883-1971) moved her millinery and dress shop to Paris, where her fashion designs and perfume continue to influence twentieth-century fashion.

*1914-1956--Babe Didrikson Zaharias, over four decades, earned more medals, set more records, and swept more tournaments in more sports than any other athlete, male or female, of the twentieth century.

1915--Lady Grace Mackenzie, explorer and filmmaker who penetrated far into the African jungle, made a highly praised documentary, Heart of Africa.

1915--Blanche Wolf Knopf (1894-1966), with her husband Alfred, founded the publishing company of Alfred A. Knopf, Inc., and later became its director and publisher.

*1916--Jeannette Rankin (1880-1973) was the first woman elected to the United States House of Representatives when Montana selected her four years before the Nineteenth Amendment.

1916--Anita Loos (1893-1981), called by some the "O. Henrietta" of the movies, is credited with bringing a new dimension to films when she wrote titles for silent films.

1918- --Ella Fitzgerald was one of the most highly respected jazz musicians of her era.

1918--Christabel Pankhurst, the eldest daughter of Emmeline, ran for Parliament in the first election after women were given the vote in Great Britain--but lost.

1918- --Pablita Velarde is a painter and illustrator of traditional American Indian earth art.

1919--Mary Pickford (1893-1970), Hollywood's first superstar, formed United Artists with D. W. Griffith, Charlie Chaplin, and Douglas Fairbanks. By 1932, she had become one of the richest self-made women in America.

*1920--The Nineteenth Amendment, giving women the right to vote, was passed.

1920--Ada Lewis Sawyer, through a Rhode Island Supreme Court decision ruling that a woman was a person, became the first woman admitted to the Rhode Island bar.

1920--Maud Wood Park (1871-1955) was the first national president of the League of Women Voters. In 1924, she organized the Women's Joint Congressional Committee, a lobbying front.

*1920--Jane Addams (1860-1935) was instrumental in forming the American Civil Liberties Union.

1920s and 30s--Jovita Gonzales was one of the first Chicanas to write in English about the Chicano culture.

1921--British author Agatha Christie (1891-1976), the most widely translated writer in the English language, began her 55-year literary career.

1922--Rebecca Ann Latimer Felton (1835-1930) was the first woman to be seated in the United States Senate.

1922--Judith Cary Waller (1889-1973) became the first station-master of one of the first and largest radio stations in the United States, the Chicago Daily News's WGU, which used the call letters WMAQ.

1923--Alice Paul (1885-1977) drafted the original Equal Rights Amendment.

1924--Ora Washington became the first black woman to win the American Tennis Association singles title, which she held for twelve years--longer than any other woman for any tournament in tennis history.

1925--Nellie Tayloe Ross (1876-1977), of Wyoming, was the first woman governor.

*1925--Florence Rena Sabin (1871-1953), an anatomist, was the first woman elected to the National Academy of Sciences.

1926--Karen Danielssen Horney (1885-1952), a psychoanalyst, began writing articles that rejected manifestations of male bias in psychoanalytic theory.

1926--Gertrude Bell (1868-1926), British archaeologist, organized the Iraq Museum, which is now one of the finest repositories of antiquities in the world.

1926--Lotte Reiniger (1899-   ), German, created the first full-length animated film--The Adventures of Prince Achmed.

1926--Ann Lowe (1898-   ) became the first black dress designer.

1927- --Leontyne Price, a soprano, was the first black
singer to have a leading role in a Metropolitan Opera
premiere (1961) and the first opera star to receive the
Presidential Medal of Freedom (1964).

1927--Mei-ling Chiang (Mme. Chiang Kai-shek; 1898-), director of the New Life Movement in China, has been
called "the brains of China," "Madame Dictator," and
"the first lady of China."

1929--Dorothy Arzner (1900-1979) was the first woman director of cinema during the transition from silents to talk-
ies and the only professional woman director to have
a regular place in Hollywood.

1928?- --Sarah Caldwell, an opera producer, director, and
conductor, is often referred to as the "first lady of
American opera."

1930--Amalie Noether (1882-1935), in the words of Albert
Einstein, "was the most significant creative mathemat-
ical genius thus far produced since the higher education of women began."

1931--Democrat Hattie Wyatt Caraway (1878-1950) became the
first woman elected to the United States Senate. In
1932, she became the first woman to preside over the
Senate.

*1931--Jane Addams became the first woman to receive the
Nobel Peace Prize.

1932--Dorothy Garrod led the joint archaeological expedition
that discovered "Mount Carmel man" in Israel.

1933--Nellie Tayloe Ross became the first woman director
of the United States Bureau of the Mint.

1933--Rose Schneiderman (1882-1972), a union organizer and
president of the Women's Trade Union League in the
1920s, became the first and only woman member of
the National Recovery Administration's Labor Advisory
Board.

*1933--Frances Perkins (1882-1965), the first woman ever
named to the President's Cabinet in the United States,
was Franklin D. Roosevelt's Secretary of Labor.

*1933--Mary McLeod Bethune (1875-1955), the founder and first president of a college for black girls (the Daytona Normal and Industrial School for Training Negro Girls), was the only black woman adviser to President Franklin D. Roosevelt.

*1935--Irene Joliot-Curie (1897-1956), continuing the work of her mother, Marie Curie, discovered a technique for making certain elements radioactive; she and her husband were awarded the Nobel Prize for Chemistry.

1935--Edith Wharton (1862-1937) became the first woman to win the Pulitzer Prize twice--first for The Age of Innocence (1920) and second for The Old Maid (1935).

*1935--Anthropologist Margaret Mead (1901-1978) supplied evidence to support the theory that social relations and culture--not anatomy--are the major determinants of human behavior.

1937--Anne O'Hare McCormick (1882-1954) became the first woman to be awarded a major Pulitzer Prize in journalism.

1937--Helen Sioussat, who succeeded Edward R. Murrow, became the top woman network executive for CBS.

*1937--Amelia Earhart (1897-1937) was the first woman to cross the Atlantic by plane (1928), first to fly solo across the Atlantic (1932), first to fly from Hawaii to California (1935), and first to attempt a round-the-world flight.

1938--Pennsylvanian Crystal Bird Fauset (1894-1965) became the first black woman elected to a state legislature in the United States.

1938--Margaret Fogarty Rudkin (1897-1967), baking her first loaf of bread at the age of forty, launched Pepperidge Farm, her famous multimillion-dollar baking company after starting her business at home.

1938--Genevieve Caulfield (1888-), blind from infancy, established the Bangkok School for the Blind.

1939--Anna Mary Moses (Grandma Moses) (1860-1961) began her career as a primitive painter when she was in her seventies.

1940--Hattie McDaniel (1898-1952) was the first black performer to win an Academy Award, for Best Supporting Actress, in Gone with the Wind (1939).

1940--Dale Messick (1906-) was virtually the only woman to create and maintain a major newspaper comic strip--"Brenda Starr, Reporter."

1941--Australian soprano Marjorie Lawrence (1908-1979) courageously returned to the stage for several years, singing from a camouflaged wheelchair, after she was stricken with infantile paralysis.

*1942--Maria Tallchief (1925-) was the first American Indian to be honored as a prima ballerina in ballet.

1943-1947--Dr. Leona Marshall Libby (1919-) was a prominent member of the Manhattan District group of scientists who built the first nuclear reactor.

1943--Private Minnie Spotted-Wolf (1923-), who enlisted in the Marine Corps Women's Reserve, was the first full-blooded Indian recruit.

1943- --Helen Hardin, a Pueblo, is a contemporary American Indian artist known for her acrylics.

*1944--Anne Frank (1929-1945), while hiding from the Nazis, wrote a diary that showed the courage, feelings, hopes, and dreams of a teenage girl under persecution.

1945--Doris Fleeson (1901-1970) was the first syndicated woman political columnist.

1945--Georgette "Dickey" Meyer Chapelle (1920-1965), combat photographer and correspondent, covered 20 years of wars and revolutions.

1947--Anna Weinstock was the first woman federal mediator.

1947--Ann Baumgartner Carl became the first woman ever to fly a jet plane.

1947--Dr. Ethel Percy Andrus (1884-1967) was the founder of the National Retired Teachers Association and the American Association of Retired Persons.

1949--Eugenie Moore Anderson (1909-) was appointed

President Harry S. Truman's ambassador to Denmark, making her the first United States woman ambassador.

1949--Simone de Beauvoir (1908-) wrote The Second Sex, which set an important intellectual precedent for the new feminism.

1950--Gwendolyn Brooks (1917-), who wrote Annie Allen, was the first black woman to receive the Pulitzer Prize.

*1951--Annie Dodge Wauneka, a Navajo, became the first woman elected to the Navajo Tribal Council.

1953--Jacqueline Cochran (1910?-1980) of the United States became the first woman to exceed the speed of sound. In 1960, she was the first woman to fly at Mach 2 (twice the speed of sound).

1953--Oveta Culp Hobby (1905-), a lawyer and politician, became the first Secretary of Health, Education, and Welfare in the Cabinet of President Dwight D. Eisenhower.

1953--Clare Boothe Luce (1903-), appointed by President Dwight D. Eisenhower, served as United States ambassador to Italy, the first American woman ambassador to a major power.

*1954--Laura Ingalls Wilder (1867-1957) was the first recipient of the Laura Ingalls Wilder Award, which was created to honor "an author or illustrator whose books published in the United States have over a period of years made a lasting contribution to literature for children."

1955--Marian Anderson (1902-) was the first black soloist of the Metropolitan Opera.

1955--Rosa Parks (1913-) refused to "move to the rear" of a Montgomery, Alabama, bus, triggering a bus boycott led by Martin Luther King, Jr., which marked a turning point in the history of black protest. She became known as the "mother of the civil-rights movement."

1956--Larissa Latynina, a Russian gymnast in the 1956, 1960, and 1964 Olympics, holds the all-time record total of

18 Olympic medals (six individual and three team gold medals, five silver, and four bronze).

1956--Bette Clair Nesmith Graham, founder of the Liquid Paper Corporation, developed the idea of "painting out" typing errors in her kitchen.

1957--Helen Meyer, president and later chairwoman of the Board of Dell Publishing Co., Inc., was the only woman to be operating head of a major publishing house.

1959--Sirimavo Bandaranaike (1916-), of Sri Lanka, became the world's first woman prime minister.

1959--Mary Leakey found the Olduvai skull, the "missing link" in human evolution from the apes, although her husband, Louis B. Leakey, is generally credited with the find.

1960--Nancy Dickerson (1929?-) became the first woman TV correspondent at CBS (1960), the first woman to have a daily network TV news program for NBC (1963), and the first woman in television to report from the floor of a national political convention.

*1960--Wilma Rudolph (1940-), called the Black Gazelle, overcame illness and a crippled leg to become the first and only American woman to win three gold medals in track and field events at a single Olympics.

1960s--Dolores Huerta (1930-) became the vice president of the United Farm Workers Union, a lobbyist, and chief negotiator for Cesar Chavez.

*1961--Emily Pauline Johnson (1861-1913) was the first author and the first Indian to appear on a Canadian postage stamp.

1961--Elizabeth Gurley Flynn (1890-1964) was the first woman to be chosen chairperson of the national committee of the Communist Party of the United States.

*1961-1979--Billie Jean King (1943-), of the United States, has won more matches (203) and more titles (20: six singles, ten doubles, and four mixed doubles) than any other player in Wimbledon's history.

*1962--Marine biologist Rachel Carson (1907-1964), in her
book Silent Spring, alerted the English-reading world
to the destructive effects of pesticides.

1963--Bessie Margolin and Morag McLeod Simchak coauthored
the Equal Pay Act, which was intended to aid the
woman worker and to establish a federal standard of
equal pay for equal work.

*1963--Valentina Vladimirovna Tereshkova-Nikolayeva (1937-   ),
of Russia, became the first woman to orbit the earth
in space.

1963-1968--President Johnson appointed women to agencies
that had never before had women members--the Atomic
Energy Commission (Mary I. Bunting), the Interstate
Commerce Commission (Virginia Mae Brown), and the
Equal Employment Opportunities Commission (Aileen
Hernandez).

1964--Fannie Lou Hamer (1918-1977), cofounder of the Mississippi Democratic Party, challenged the all-white
regular Mississippi delegation to the Democratic National Convention and became one of the most powerful
leaders of the civil-rights movement.

1964--Margaret Chase Smith (1897-   ) was the first woman
ever placed in nomination for President at a major
party convention.

1964--Marlene Sanders (1931-   ) became the first woman to
anchor a network-television news show.

1965--June Brown of the Detroit News is one of the few black
women in the United States writing a regular column
for a major daily newspaper.

1965--British Sheila Scott completed the longest consecutive
solo flight by flying 31,000 miles around the world.

1966--Virginia Johnson (1925-   )--in collaboration with her
husband, Dr. William Masters--wrote Human Sexual
Response, which undermined the Freudian theory that
women should assume a passive sexual role and the
notion that women were anatomically inferior to men.
They were the first researchers to study the physiology
of sexual response.

1966--Constance Baker Motley (1921-   ) was appointed the first black woman to sit as a federal judge.

1966--Betty Friedan (1921-   ), founder and first president of the National Organization for Women (NOW), has been called "the mother of the new feminist movement."

1967--Dr. Mary L. Gambrell (1898-1974) became the first woman president of a major coeducational college, Hunter College of the City University of New York.

1967--Kathrine Switzer, a world-class long-distance runner, became the first woman ever to run in the United States famed Boston Marathon. In 1972, she became the first woman to run officially and legally in the Boston Marathon.

1967--Jo Freeman (1945-   ) organized the first consciousness-raising group, in Chicago.

1967--Chicago feminists Jo Freeman, Shulamith Firestone, Heather Booth, and Naomi Weisstein founded the first independent women's caucus organized strictly around women's issues since the fight for suffrage.

1967--Alicia Escalante formed the East Los Angeles Welfare Rights Organization, the first Chicano welfare-rights group.

1968--Charlene Mitchell, New York, presidential nominee of the Communist Party, was the first black woman nominated for the presidency.

1968--Robyn Smith (1944-   ) won the right to become a race rider. In 1973, she was the first woman jockey to win a major stakes race--at Aqueduct.

1968--Joan Ganz Cooney (1929-   ) founded the Children's Television Workshop, which produced "Sesame Street" and "The Electric Company," educational programs for children.

*1969--Shirley Chisholm (1924-   ), Democratic representative from New York, was the first black woman elected to Congress.

1969--Denise Long was drafted by the San Francisco Warriors, a professional basketball team.

1970s--These years will be remembered as the breakthrough years for women in politics and government. No decade in history has had more significant gains of "firsts" for women in public life.

1970--Anne Thompson became the first black woman prosecutor in the United States in Lawrence, New Jersey.

1970--Marie Cox founded the North American Indian Women's Association, the first national group for Indian women, and was chosen by that group as Outstanding Indian Woman of 1977.

1970--LaDonna Harris, an active member of the Comanche Indian tribe, was the founder and president of Americans for Indian Opportunity, whose primary purpose was to work toward improving the quality of life for Native Americans.

1970--Margaret E. Kuhn (1905-) founded the Gray Panthers, an activist group fighting ageism.

1970--Anna Mae Hayes and Elizabeth P. Hoisington of the army became the first female generals in the armed services.

1971--The National Women's Political Caucus, an organization dedicated to thrusting women into positions of power at all levels of government, was formed by Congresswoman Bella Abzug, Gloria Steinem, Betty Friedan, and Fannie Lou Hamer.

1971--Elma Barrera organized the First National Chicana Conference.

1972--Sally Preisand was ordained as the first woman rabbi in the United States and the world.

1972--Captain Arlene B. Duerk (1921-) became the first woman admiral in the history of the United States Navy.

1972--Cecily Cannan Selby (1927-) became the first woman ever to be elected to the board of directors of Avon Products, Inc. Although Avon was founded in 1886, it was not until 1972 that women were brought into the previously all-male officer ranks of the world's largest cosmetics company.

1972--Gloria Steinem (1936?-), a freelance writer who emerged in the 1960s as a leader in the Women's Movement, cofounded Ms. magazine, with Patricia Carbine as publisher and editor-in-chief.

1972--Frances "Sissy" Farenthold (1926-) was the first woman to have her name placed in nomination--in a spontaneous draft--for the vice presidency of the United States.

*1972--Shirley Chisholm, of New York, became the first black woman presidential nominee of a major party.

1972--Martha Griffiths (1912-), Congresswoman from Michigan, devised the strategy that got the Equal Rights Amendment out of committee and through Congress.

1972--Carmen Maymi, Paquita Vivo, and others organized the National Conference of Puerto Rican Women, in Washington.

1972--Jean Westwood was selected chair of the Democratic National Committee--the first woman to hold that position in either party.

1972--Eleanor Rigor (1929-) became a sports producer for ABC, the first female TV sports producer.

1972--Romana Acosta Banuelos (1925-), a prominent Mexican-American businesswoman from Los Angeles, was appointed and confirmed as the Treasurer of the United States.

1973--Judy Lilly was the top super stock drag racer in the United States.

1973--Mary Daly (1928-), radical feminist and theologian, wrote The Church and the Second Sex and Beyond God the Father (1974), which explore the antifemale bias and patriarchal language in the Roman Catholic Church and society.

1973--The National Black Feminist Organization was formed with the goal of helping black women achieve a positive identity while also combating the oppression of all black people.

1973--Emily Howell became the first woman crew member of a certified United States airline.

1973--Angelita Rosal (1956-   ), a Sioux table-tennis player, was the first Indian woman inducted into the American Indian Athletic Hall of Fame in Lawrence, Kansas.

1973--Lorelei Means (1951-   ) and Madonna Gilbert (1937-   ), both Lakota (or Sioux) Indians, opened the "We Will Remember" Survival School in Rapid City, South Dakota, to offer an educational alternative for Indian children.

1973--The United States Supreme Court ruled that women had a constitutional right to abortion during the first six months of pregnancy.

1974--Ella Grasso (1919-1981) was elected governor of Connecticut, the first woman governor in United States history who did not follow her husband into office.

1974--Lucy--the oldest, most complete, and best-preserved skeleton of any erect-walking human ancestor ever found--was discovered by Donald Johanson in the Afar region of Ethiopia.

1974--The Mexican American Women's Association (MAWA) was founded.

1974--The National Women's Football League was formed.

1974--Maria Estela M. de Peron (Isabel Peron) (1931-   ) of Argentina became the first woman president in the world, following the death of her husband.

1974--Janet Gray Hayes, from San Jose, California, was the first woman elected mayor of a large United States city.

1974--Lorene Rogers (1914-   ) was appointed president of the University of Texas (Austin), the first woman president of a major university.

*1974--The Little League was forced to franchise teams for girls in baseball.

1974--The Coalition of Labor Union Women (CLUW) was formed to improve the status of all working women and marked the first time that United States women coalesced on a nationwide basis.

1974--Lanny Moss was the first woman to manage any baseball league team.

1974--Dorothy Richey, director of athletics at Chicago State
University, became the first woman to hold that position
at a coeducational institution.

1975--The International Women's Year conference in Mexico
City stressed the need for women's participation in
government and set goals for increased literacy, employment, and civic, social, and political equality.

1975--Carla Anderson Hills (1934-   ) became the first woman
Secretary of Housing and Urban Development.

1975--Joellen Drag was the Navy's first woman helicopter
pilot.

1975--Congress passed a bill requiring the service academies
to admit women.

1975--Betty Southard Murphy was appointed the first chairwoman of the National Labor Relations Board.

1975--Junko Tabei, member and deputy leader of an all-women
Japanese expedition, became the first woman in the
world to scale Mount Everest, the highest mountain on
earth.

1975--Billie Jean King, Joan Joyce, and Janie Blalock organized the Women's Pro Softball League.

1975--Susie M. Sharp of North Carolina became the first
woman elected chief justice of a state supreme court.

1976--Rosalind Franklin, geneticist, was noted for her work
in solving the riddle of the DNA molecule.

1976--Captain Vittoria Renzullo became the first woman to
command a New York City police precinct.

*1976--Janet Guthrie (1938-   ), of the United States, became
the first woman driver to qualify for the Indianapolis
500.

*1976--American Kitty O'Neil (1948?-   ), deaf since birth,
holds the women's world land-speed record of 612 m.p.h.

1977--Linda Snyder, blind and partially deaf since birth, received her law degree from Georgetown University Law School, Washington, D. C.

1977--Patricia Roberts Harris (1924-), the highest-ranking woman lawyer in United States government, was the first black woman appointed to a President's Cabinet (Secretary of Housing and Urban Development) and the first to be named an American ambassador (to Luxembourg).

1977--Juanita M. Kreps (1921-) became the first woman Secretary of Commerce in the United States.

1977--Betty Cook (1923-) became the open-class world champion in offshore powerboat racing. In 1981, she won her third national title.

1977--Rosalie Muschal Reinhardt became the first married woman to have completed all the academic requirements for admission to the Roman Catholic priesthood.

1977--Barbara Walters (1931-) was the first woman to co-anchor a network evening news program and, at a million dollars a year, the highest-paid journalist in history.

1977--The first national power-lifting competition for women was held in Nashua, New Hampshire.

1977--Eleanor Holmes Norton (1937-), a black lawyer who was the first woman head of the New York Human Rights Commission, became the first woman to chair the Equal Employment Opportunities Commission.

1977--Kim Peters, chosen for Parade magazine's first All American High School Girls' Basketball Team, was born without a right hand and was acknowledged to be the finest defensive player in her home state of Iowa.

1978--Louise Brown, the world's first "test-tube" baby, was born in England.

*1978--Harriet Tubman was the first black woman to be depicted on a United States postage stamp.

1978--The Women's Professional Basketball League was formed.

*1978--Naomi James (1949-) was the first woman to com-
plete a round-the-world ocean voyage solo.

1978--The first women astronauts were selected--Dr. Anne
L. Fisher (1950-), Dr. Shannon W. Lucid (1943-),
Dr. Judith A. Resnik (1950-), Sally K. Ride (1951-
), Dr. Margaret R. Seddon, and Kathryn D. Sullivan
(1952-).

*1978--Nancy Lopez (1957-) was named the Ladies Profes-
sional Golf Association Rookie and Player of the Year.

1979--Beverly Kelley became the first woman to command a
United States military vessel.

1979--The Women's Hall of Fame--containing sketches and
memorabilia of women who have made contributions
to the arts, sports, business, education, government,
and science--was established in Seneca Falls, New
York.

1979--Margaret Thatcher (1925-), the first woman party
leader in British history, became Britain's first
woman Prime Minister.

*1979--Susan B. Anthony was the first real woman to appear
on a United States coin.

1979--Maria de Lourdes Pintassilgo was named Portugal's
first woman Prime Minister.

1979--Sonia Johnson, of Sterling, Virginia, was excommun-
icated from the Church of Jesus Christ of Latter-day
Saints for allegedly preaching false doctrine, under-
mining church authority, and hurting missionary efforts
when she publicly supported the Equal Rights Amendment.

1979--Beverly Sills (1929-), an outstanding coloratura soprano, became general director of the New York City
Opera.

1980--Carolyn Farrell (1935-), was the first nun to be mayor
of an American city--Dubuque, Iowa.

*1980--Kateri Tekakwitha, known as "the Lily of the Mo-
hawks," an Iroquois Indian who lived in the middle

seventeenth century, was the first North American Indian to be elevated to the status of "blessed," one step below sainthood, in the Roman Catholic Church.

1980--Vigdis Finnbogadottir, the world's first freely elected woman head of state, was elected President of Iceland.

1980--Andrea Jaeger (1965-), at 15 years of age, was the youngest player ever to be seeded in the Wimbledon tennis tournament.

1980--Nancy Landon Kassebaum (1932-), of Kansas, was the first woman to win election to the Senate in her own right.

1980--Debbie Hart was ordained into the males-only Mormon priesthood by her husband to protest the church's opposition to the Equal Rights Amendment.

1980--Janice Brown was the first person to pilot a sustained flight solar-powered flying machine, the Gossamer Penguin.

1981--Astronaut Kathryn Sullivan and diver Sylvia Earle became the first female Explorers admitted to the 75-year-old Explorers Club in Manhattan.

1981--Mother Angelica founded the first FCC-licensed TV station for a monastical order in Irondale, Alabama-- the Eternal Word Television Network.

1981--Zofia Grzyb, a shoe-factory supervisor, became the first woman on the ruling Polish Politburo.

1981--Kathy Rinaldi (1967-), at 14, became the youngest tennis player to win a match at Wimbledon and the youngest professional in tennis history.

1981--Raquel Martinez, in Tijuana, Mexico, became the first woman to achieve professional status in a major bull-ring.

1981--Sandra Day O'Connor (1930-), judge on the Arizona Court of Appeals, was the first woman appointed to the United States Supreme Court.

Great Britain, 156, 158, 167,
170, 224, 237, 359, 360,
362, 416, 460, 480, 507
Scotland, 236, 357, 358
Suffrage, 224, 344
Great Gilly Hopkins, The, 301
Great Pete Penney, The, 349
Green, Phyllis, 243, 244, 245
Greenberg, Barbara, 50
Greene, Bette, 381, 439
Greene, Constance C., 246,
247
Greenfield, Eloise, 382, 514
Greenwald, Sheila, 51, 248,
249, 250
Greta the Strong, 336
Grifalconi, Ann, 52
Griffin, Judith Berry, 515
Groman, Gal, 251
Guerin, Mrs. E. J., 485
Guthrie, Janet, 467, 485
Guy, Rosa, 383

Haas, Irene, 53
Hahn, Emily, 495
Haley, Gail E., 54
Hall, Elizabeth, 252
Hall, Lynn, 253
Hall, Rosalys, 55
Halloween Pumpkin Smasher,
The, 124
Hamilton, Alice, 484
Hamilton, Virginia, 401
Handicapped (see Mental Illness,
Mentally Handicapped, Physi-
cally Handicapped)
Hang On, Hester!, 34
Hann, Jacquie, 56
Hapgood, Miranda, 57
Harler, Anne, 451
Harmelink, Barbara, 477
Harriet and the Promised Land,
510
Harriet and the Runaway Book:
The Story of Harriet Beecher
Stowe and Uncle Tom's
Cabin, 452
Harriet the Spy, 230
Harris, Christie, 254
Hart, Carole, 58
Hartley, Lucie, 528
Haskins, James, 516, 517

Hassler, Jon, 402
Haunting of Julie Unger, The,
284
Have You Seen Wilhelmina
Krumpf?, 22
Hayes, Kent, 255
Haynes, Betsy, 384
Hazen, Barbara Shook, 256
He Bear, She Bear, 11
Hearing Impaired (see Physically
Handicapped)
Heidish, Marcy, 518
Helga's Dowry: A Troll Love
Story, 31
Heller, Linda, 59
Henrietta and the Day of the
Iguana, 120
Henrietta and the Gong from
Hong Kong, 120
Henrietta, the Wild Woman of
Borneo, 120
Henry Reed, Inc., 316
Henry Reed's Babysitting Service,
316
Henry Reed's Big Show, 316
Henry Reed's Journey, 316
Herstory: A Woman's View of
American History, 499
Hester the Jester, 128
Hew Against the Grain, 219
Hey, Wait for Me! I'm Amelia,
45
Highland Rebel, 357
Hildick, E. W., 257, 258
Hilgartner, Beth, 259
Hill, Donna, 60
Himler, Ronald, 61
Hirsh, Marilyn, 62
Hoban, Russell, 63
Hocken, Sheila, 536
Holland, Isabelle, 418
Holtzman, Elizabeth, 486
Homeward the Arrow's Flight,
522
Honestly, Katie John!, 194
Hook a Fish, Catch a Mountain,
239
Hoover, H. M., 260, 419
Hornet's Nest, The, 358
Horses, 101, 196, 253, 290,
291, 307, 393, 442
Horvath, Betty, 64
Hot Day, The, 51

Rabe, Berniece, 312, 313
Rachel and Obadiah, 429
Rachel's Legacy, 435
Rafiki, 79
Rain Rain Rivers, 129
Rankin, Jeannette, 486
Raskin, Ellen, 314
Real Me, The, 286
Reavin, Sam, 115
Rebel on a Rock, 168
Red Hart Magic, 295
Red Rock over the River, 396
Reed, Tom, 116
Reesink, Marijke, 117
Religion, 200, 464, 470, 498,
523
Revolt of 10-X, The, 198
Rice, Edward, 493
Richard, Adrienne, 315
Richter, Alice Numeroff, 108
Riedman, Sarah R., 494
Rinehart Lifts, 266
Rita the Weekend Rat, 280
Roberta Flack, 519
Robertson, Keith, 316
Robinson, Nancy K., 317
Robison, Nancy, 118, 539
Rockwell, Anne, 119
Roll of Thunder, Hear My Cry,
392
Roosevelt, Eleanor, 498
Rosen, Winifred, 120
Rosie and Michael, 139
Ross, Diana, 517
Ross, Jessica, 121
Ross, Pat, 495
Rothman, Joel, 122
Ruby, 3
Run Don't Walk, 426
Runaway to Freedom: A Story
of the Underground Railway,
390
Running Away from Home, 23,
25, 78, 117, 150, 186, 270,
287, 340, 341, 415, 423

Sabin, Florence, 484
Sacagawea, 534
Sacagawea: The Story of an
American Indian, 534
Sachs, Marilyn, 318, 319,
320, 321

Saint (see Religion)
St. George, Judith, 123, 124,
322
St. John, Wylly Folk, 323
Saito, Michiko, 125
Salted Lemons, 331
Sam, 214
Sanger, Margaret, 495
Sara and the Door, 66
Sarah Bishop, 297
Sarah Somebody, 444
Sargent, Shirley, 324
Sarton, May, 325
Saving of P.S., The, 186
Savitz, Harriet May, 426
Schlein, Miriam, 126
School Problems, 86, 180, 214,
222, 223, 245, 281, 286,
294, 305, 317, 321, 327,
353, 355, 356, 365, 381,
387, 391, 412, 444, 447
Schulman, Janet, 127
Science Fiction, 163, 221, 233,
234, 260, 293, 294, 295,
332, 343, 388, 389, 419,
420
Scientists, 466, 469, 472, 484,
489, 491, 492, 493, 494,
496, 500, 504
Sea and Earth: The Life of
Rachel Carson, 500
Sea Stories, 53, 81, 93, 115,
132, 366, 479
Secret Dinosaur, The, 62
Secret of the Emerald Star, 364
Secret of the Strawbridge Place,
The, 262
Secret of Van Rink's Cellar, The,
278
Secret Summer of L.E.B., The,
355
Selfridge, Oliver G., 326
Senior Citizens, 166, 191, 244,
261, 287, 309, 325, 415
Series Books, 2, 10, 23, 24,
26, 27, 37, 41, 63, 87, 88,
95, 120, 156, 157, 158, 161,
178, 179, 188, 194, 199,
202, 212, 217, 230, 251,
257, 258, 262, 266, 272,
282, 289, 304, 307, 316,
321, 327, 332, 339, 344,
367, 381, 403, 406, 412,